Li
Think **LARGE.**
Act **SENSIBLY.**

How to make a fortune - without losing your friends!

NICK JAMES

Live **BIG.** Think **LARGE.** Act **SENSIBLY.**

How to make a fortune - without losing your friends!

First published 2007

POWER-TECH
Associates Limited

ISBN 0-9554865-0-5   ISBN 978-0-9554865-0-0

The author can be contacted at the address below or by email at nick@nick-james.com

First published 2007 by
Power-Tech Associates Limited
5 Forest Court, Oaklands Park,
Wokingham, Berkshire, RG41 2FD
United Kingdom.

Tel: 0845 117 3000
Fax: 0845 117 4000
www.Nick-James.com

Printed in Great Britain by the MPG Books Group, Bodmin and King's Lynn

Content

Introduction

SOME people dream about making money. Lots of it. It obsesses them every waking hour of every working day. Some people talk about making lots of money. Endlessly. They talk and talk and talk. And you know what - that's all they ever do. Just talk.

Then there are the others. These are the special kind of people. Special, because they don't just talk. They don't just think. They think and talk, they plan and act ... and they do.

The brilliant English playwright Harold Pinter captured most people you will ever meet quite beautifully in his stark play, The Caretaker, which he loaded with menacing reality. The cry of the down and out Davies was: "If I could only get to Sidcup."

Pinter's point was achingly brilliant. Here was a man, a character in a play who stood for every man or woman that you've ever met who talked big, or thought big, but who never, ever did. Never took the action. Never took hold of their dreams. Didn't really want what they obsessed over ... and were not prepared to pay the price to get it. Grasp a nettle and it stings, unless someone shows you how to do it without getting stung.

Pinter's down and out character Davies was never going to get to Sidcup. His life would be played out in the most ordinary circumstances and he would remain obsessed and unfulfilled until he drew his last breath. Always wanting. Always longing. But without a hope of ever "getting there" because he didn't want it hard enough!

When I sat down to write this book, I remembered Harold Pinter's play.

You see success does not come cheap. And in the words of the great American playwright, Arthur Miller, **everything comes at a price.**

The question I have to ask you - and I want you to pause right here, right now before you answer - is this: **are you prepared to pay the price?**

Do you truly want to get to Sidcup?

You do? Then walk with me. Our journey begins.

Chapter 1

Where it begins

"Judge your success by what you had to give up to get it."

I DON'T really know who actually said that, but I have remembered it for a very long time. Chain mail folklore tries to convince us that it was the Dalai Lama. The truth is that H Jackson Brown Jr probably coined it in his excellent little manual *Life's Little Instruction Book.*

Who actually wrote this isn't the issue. It's the point he is making that is cased in gold. You see, everything does come at a price and I ought to know - *because I've paid it!*

You wake up one morning. You're laughing and joking with your workmates, your friends, family or colleagues. You're at a ball game, watching soccer, cornered down on the train, squashed on the tube, walking the dog or playing with kids.

And it hits you. Plain, dead centre. You don't want to live like this, anymore.

Some would call it an epiphany. Me, I simply call it an awakening. Something, someone, some event has thrummed the strings of your life and your head starts playing to a different tune. And it's a persistent little ditty because it changes everything and alters the whole way you look at your life.

It alters what you will accept, it transforms what you want out of life and it redefines the way you are going to set about acquiring it. If you let it, it creates a whole new you. But you have to let it breathe and allow it to work its own special kind of magic.

Remember what I said at the top of the page: you must *judge your success by what you had to give up to get it.*

Remember that and keep it close by. As your success unfolds it will serve as a reminder to you. It will keep your feet on the ground, your sanity in place and give you the reality check that, at some time or another, we all need.

Did I say magic? Aren't we a little too old and a lot too long in the tooth for that? Don't you believe it! Sometimes, things just happen. There's no particular reason, no special justification, no science. It "just happens"! Period. Roll with it. Go with it and I tell you great things can and do happen. Magic. Chance. Luck. Good fortune. Call it what you will, but I can tell you to trust it … because I know that it works.

Not that long ago, I was in Dead End Alley. Going nowhere. No plan, no hope and not really any dreams, either. And I'd never been near Sidcup!

I was a two-bit car park attendant with debts longer than I am (I'm well over six feet!), bills flying in and no hope of paying them off until probably long after I was dead! It was a scary kind of stultifyingly dull and monotonously grey life.

I was living a nothing life with very little money, no prospects and marriage that was slithering down the pan. But who wants to help you when you're down there?

Then I got woken up. A friend persuaded me, somewhat

reluctantly, to go with him to a seminar at London's Heathrow airport, to hear a man "give up the secrets to enormous wealth".

No doubt you've heard that one too? By this time, I'm middle twenties and tell him that I'm just too old for fairy tales. In time-honoured fashion, we make a bet and it comes down to the simple toss of a coin: heads I go to the seminar, tails I go to work.

Yes, I "lost" and off I went to hear this "great man speak".

What I heard totally changed my life! Quite honestly, it was the smartest move that I think I have ever made.

I heard a man, a direct marketing wizard, give up the secrets to making yourself very wealthy. Very wealthy indeed. And what I heard that day, totally changed my life. I could hardly afford the time off work because money-wise things were so very tight, but I took it and I have been grateful ever since.

How about that? Still don't believe in magic, luck, good fortune, fate or whatever you personally want to call it? Sometimes, as Darth Vader constantly reminds us, it pays just occasionally to allow yourself to *"give in to the Dark Side"!*

So I was dragged kicking, screaming and moaning loudly in my friend's ear all the way to London Heathrow. And what happened there was a revelation to me. Not so much the words and content given out over the course of the seminar. But for the very first time, I could see a structure emerging that would shape the whole of the rest of my life.

Right there, in a crowded conference room, my dreams

started to crystallise and I could see Nirvana, the Holy Grail and the Promised Land - the whole shooting match! What's more, I had been shown how to get there!

I had a plan and a route map. I was up and off and ready and you know what? Even though I now drive an Aston Martin - I've still never been anywhere near Sidcup!

What's the significance of my story? Everything has to start somewhere and sometimes things happen for no justifiable reason. They just do. Be open to that. Accept it, roll with it, run with it and profit from it. And most of all - be glad that you did!

I hope in so many ways that this book will prove to be your own wake up call. The plain truth is that everybody needs somebody to help them "get there" because in the words of the rock legend Bruce Springsteen: *"You can't get there on your own!"*

He needed a band (and it is a mighty fine band too!). In my own way, I too have a band. A band of associates, helpers, suppliers and customers who all work together in a virtual city of information, offer, exchange and purchase that repeatedly makes great things happen. They're not world-changing events, but they are events of huge personal significance that inspire, enable, inform and guide people to achieve their own aims and intentions.

In a nutshell, that is what I have created since my awakening at Heathrow: a global matrix that satisfies a huge number of people's wants and needs on a regular basis. It puts answers in their hands and puts money in my pocket. Lots and lots of it.

It hasn't been easy, but it has been a lot of fun!

Still think great things can't happen for you?

Are you one of those people that wanders through life envying everyone who is better off than you? Do you genuinely either seriously or mildly despise people who are "successful"?

Do you think that life dealt you a bad hand and there's nothing you can do about it because you only hold two's and three's and everybody else holds Aces, Queens and Kings?

Is life plotting and planning against you? Is it stopping you from becoming the success you know you should be and preventing you from achieving all of the goals and dreams that you have set for yourself?

Life, eh? It can be a real pain, can't it?

Wake up! Stop this loser syndrome. Shake yourself from the Wall of Death that you have set yourself upon. Remember the old circus act, the Wall of Death? The guy rode his motorcycle round and round a cylindrical structure, faster and faster, rising ever higher and higher and the people paid to look down on him from the top of the structure. He never went anywhere. Where could he go, except round and round and round? Ad infinitum. Ad nauseum.

If that's how you see your life, you seriously need help! You need my help because I don't have time for losers and I won't allow you to ride any more on the Wall of Death!

It's time you shook off the monotony of daily drudgery. It's time you took control. It's time someone showed you the way to reach your own Promised Land.

But if you are going to waste the rest of your life hoping for that "megafix" to come along and find you in the shape of millions of pounds, dollars, yen or euros, or appear as if by magic from some place else that you've got in mind, then no one can help you. Not anyone.

You'd best stick to the Lottery and hope that the windfall finds you and gives you the wealth you believe you deserve. Sure, enormous wealth does happen occasionally, for 1 in 14 million, or so. But for most of us it is and remains a giant fairy story that is never fulfilled, however much money we throw at it.

But didn't I say something about magic, chance, luck and good fortune? Yes, I did, but I wasn't talking about what Lady Luck might throw at you! That's a whole other ball game and if it happens for you, then good luck and all power to you. For most of us, a huge windfall simply doesn't and isn't ever going to happen.

Luck on a truly obscene scale isn't what I'm talking about when I speak of magic, chance and good fortune. Here, I'm talking about that one chance that strikes you dead centre and turns your whole life around. Not a giant dose of good luck that gives you everything you could ever dream of and if you've already got that then you don't need to read any further.

Most of us haven't and won't ever get that "megafix" and it is you that I am talking to.

So, let's knock the idea on the head that a "quick fix of immensely obscene wealth" is going to fall in your lap. Chances are that it won't. Ever.

Live BIG. Think LARGE. Act SENSIBLY.
How to make a fortune - without losing your friends!

If you want wealth, you are going to have to work to earn it.

But there are two things I have to point out to you here:

1. As Tommy Lasorda, one of the most enthusiastic and successful managers in baseball history, once said: *"There are those that watch things happen, those that wonder what happened and those that make things happen."* Which of those are you?

2. Pure hard work is not and can never be the answer to reaching all of your dreams, whatever they may be. Sure hard work will take you a very long way, but hard work alone will not get you "there", wherever it is that you want to be.

As you ponder over what I've just said, I am indebted to a good friend of mine, Vince Stanzione, for giving me this little ditty, penned by Denis Waitley, one of the world's most sought after keynote speakers and productivity consultants:

> *I go to work I earn my bread*
> *I watch TV I go to bed*
> *Sunrise, sunset - year after year*
> *Before I know it, winter's here.*

You know, 95% of people in developed economies live this way. They fritter their lives in idle fantasy, live in dreams, hate successful people and despise the way they live their own lives. They most probably ALL want something better. Trouble is, they don't know how to get it and, unless it comes easily, they are not prepared to make the effort ... they are not prepared to pay the price.

Don't allow another day to fritter idly by! Not one more! Not

Live **BIG**. Think **LARGE**. Act **SENSIBLY**.
How to make a fortune - without losing your friends!

now, not ever.

Turn the page and start your own new chapter. Make today, this very moment, right here, right now, the start for you of something a whole lot better. The life you want and the realisation of your dreams is within your grasp. It is up to you to seize the moment.

What you have to ask yourself as you look around you at people who already have what you want or who are well on the way to achieving everything they've ever wanted is simply this:

What do they have that you don't - yet?

What do you think it is?

Well, I'll tell you. They have these key elements that are absolutely essential - no, more than that, they are critical - to your success:

1. Belief.
2. Determination.
3. Courage.
4. Conviction.
5. Humility.
6. A rapacious need for knowledge - *and results!*
7. The ability to completely "empty your cup".
8. A plan.
9. A dream.
10. A destination.

There is a certain humility in my point number seven and all of the great men that I have ever met have possessed this singular ability - the ability to completely "empty your cup".

I cannot and do not claim ownership of this remarkable

insight. It was taught to me in a fabulous book called *Zen in the Martial Arts* by martial arts expert Joe Hyams.

In this wonderful short book on the art of life, self-management and consummate control, Joe Hyams tells the story of the martial arts legend Bruce Lee.

Through the practice of martial arts, Bruce Lee learned many things about how to martial your own personal resources and use time efficiently. He was notoriously choosy about whom he would work with - regardless of how much money they had to spend or how enthusiastic they were. He turned away many famous and extremely wealthy people who sought him as their tutor.

But he taught Joe Hyams a lesson he was never to forget. Joe went to Bruce to enlist him as his personal teacher. Bruce asked Joe to demonstrate his moves, to show him "all that he knew".

At the end of the demonstration Bruce told Joe that, good and competent as he was, he would have to unlearn all that he knew and start all over again.

And Bruce told Joe the story his own grand master had told him about a university professor who had come to visit the old sifu (teacher). After a few moments in the professor's company, it was clear to the sifu that the man had not come to learn anything about Zen, but had come to impress the grand master with his own knowledge and opinions.

The sifu poured the professor some tea and when the cup was full he continued pouring until the cup overflowed and the professor was forced to remark that the cup was full and no more tea would go in it.

"You are like this cup," said the sifu. *"You are full of your own opinions and speculations. How can I show you Zen unless first you empty your cup?"*

The point was not lost on Joe Hyams. He knew, as all great businessmen and women do, that in order to grow and expand as people and become successful as entrepreneurs we all have to be able at some point to "empty our cups".

We have to let go to learn more. We have to be aware of and in tune with influences from every quarter. We have to be up to speed with the world and its developments. We have to feed our minds and constantly feed our imagination. We have to free our minds of the shackles and constraints of can't, don't and won't and turn them into will, can and do.

And yes, we have to be humble enough to accept that other people can do better, will know more than we do and can show us a better or at least a different way to do things.

In this life, there is no one with nothing left to learn and often it will be people much younger than ourselves who will be showing us the way. They will be our teachers, if we can empty our cups and, with cheerful humility and the best grace possible, accept the lessons they can teach us.

Take on board the Ten Critical Elements to your success that I have given you. Make them your mantra for success. Earn the right to use them wisely and success will surely be your reward, whatever the shape and definition you put on the measure of your success.

"Nothing is impossible to a willing mind."
Books of the Han Dynasty

Chapter 2

The Ten Critical Elements to your success

"You must be the person you want to become."

IN BUSINESS, it's one thing knowing the theory, but it is quite another to put that theory to good use.

Many, many business books and an awful lot of business seminars propose to offer you knowledge and know-how. What they give you is theory, but no show how. And whichever way you look at it, unless you know how to use it, even the best map in the world won't take you anywhere!

The Ten Critical Elements to your success are offered as signposts that are meant to show you the way.

Why only ten? Ten is one of life's most significant and meaningful numbers. It's how the world works in ways that memorable and meaningful. Top Ten Tips, Top Ten Foods, Top Ten Records, Top Ten People, Top Ten Destinations and so on. And there's a reason for that and it's not just because He gave you the Ten Commandments!

The human mind works best when its tasks are broken down into small chunks that are easily manageable. If I had given you 50 Critical Elements your mind would have struggled to remember just 10 of them. You'd have juggled with a few, struggled with a few and then given up! I lose, you lose and that's not good for anyone!

But the way I see it and in all the ways I've experienced it, success comes down to these ten key elements:

1. Belief.
2. Determination.
3. Courage.
4. Conviction.
5. Humility.
6. A rapacious need for knowledge - and results!
7. The ability to completely "empty your cup".
8. A plan.
9. A dream.
10. A destination.

Let's take these ten critical factors one at a time.

1. Belief

You will get nowhere without it.

Wish I could say otherwise, but I know that I cannot. Belief is crucial to your success and it will contribute enormously to all that you can achieve and everything you can ultimately become.

Belief in yourself is the key to all that you can ever achieve or hope to ever achieve because if you don't believe in yourself how can you possibly convince anyone else to, either?

It's not that long ago that a young, wayward, black American was rampaging through the streets of Washington. He was a gang member, a young thug, a hoodlum and a lawless individual who was on a fast track either to prison, or the cemetery.

Then something happened. He got shot and still has the bullet in his leg today. His awakening call had arrived.

He changed his life, completely. He completely recoded his belief system, shedding all of his old values in the process. He remodelled himself because he found the internet and discovered his own "pathway to the promised land".

Today, that man, Stephen Pierce, is one of the world's most highly respected internet marketers, a guru who regularly makes over $100,000 US in three days or less, who has secured his own personal fortune and created the fortunes of a great many others.

Most recently, none other than the White House, America's primary seat of power, awarded him a major contract. How far this man has come from the wayward days of his misspent youth!

And if he stood in front you now and you asked him how he did it, he would simply tell you that he changed his belief system and he got what he deserved!

The simple truth is that the world is not going to wait for you. It waits for no one and the right moment is now, this very second.

It's not next week, next month, next quarter, or next year. It is right now!

Don't put it off until the "moment is right". If you do, you're categorising yourself as one of those people for whom the moment in "never quite right".

And there go your dreams, right there. They're lost in a vapour of mist and fog, a ghostly reality that has neither shape nor substance because you never allowed your dreams to become real. You were simply trying to get to Sidcup!

If you want it, you have to believe it! And what's more, you have to believe you'll get it because you deserve it.

Yes it's a positive attack on your state of mind, but if you don't believe that you're a winner then give up your seat on the train and get off the bus - and don't ask me to believe it either!

If you want something you've never had before, you have to do things you've never done before. But if you keep on doing what you've been doing all you'll ever end up with is the same thing you've already got.

It's your choice.

But you can have it, whatever it is (within achievable reality - but be reasonable ... you cannot own the moon!) - if you really believe that you deserve it.

Believe in yourself - with neither constraint nor compromise - if you really want me or anyone else to believe in you.

> *"One person with belief is equal to a force of 99 who have only interests."*
> John Stuart Mill, English philosopher & economist, 1806 - 1873

2. Determination

You'll get nowhere, absolutely nowhere, without it. That's the bald and brutal truth.

Why do you think so many people have failed? And all of history is littered with heroic, not so brave and plainly stupid failures.

People fail primarily because they give up. They fold. Why? Usually, it's because the going gets tough and it all just "gets too hard", too hard to compete and far too hard to control.

So, it's easier to walk away. Hardly a solution worth shouting about, is it? But it's the option many, if not most people, will choose when things get a little hot around the kitchen.

Let's be clear about this. Life is not a breeze. It never was and it never will be. Little that is either precious or valuable comes cheaply, or is rarely given away free. That's not how life works.

If you want it, whatever it is and whatever you hold dear, you have to be prepared to earn it - you have to prove yourself, to yourself and to others, too. That is how life works.

Look around you. Without wishing to be rude or insulting in any way to anybody, there are failures all around you and on every side. All those "coulda beens", "woulda beens" and "shoulda beens". Same old story. Same old result.

It's true what the old song's sentiment made popular by Lynn Anderson says: No one ever promised you a rose garden! Life can be hard, it can be cruel and it can be a relentless taskmaster. It can take away just as freely as it gives, but push all of that out the way.

For all its troubles, for all of its ups and downs and many injustices, life is an utterly absorbing and wholly engaging experience!

We should all rejoice every single minute of every single day in the fact that we are here! We have a life. We have the opportunity to do immense things with it. Life itself is an utterly incredible thing!

Who really knows for sure how we got here? And I am certainly not going to waste words and pages on the theory of creation versus the presence of an ever-present creator! Brains far bigger than mine have tried and seem to have done little but fan the flames with a fuel of confusion. One minute it is this - without a doubt! Then the next it's that - and there can be no reasonable doubt. Till, of course, it all changes, and once more we're asked to believe in something else that is … totally different, but still beyond any reasonable doubt!

As Charles Darwin, the father of the theory of evolution, once remarked: *"I have clung tenaciously to all my beliefs … until someone has proven otherwise!"* And I'd say hear, hear to that!

Suffice, for my purposes, to say that we are here and that in itself is an unbelievable miracle. I, for one, am immensely proud to be a member of the human race and I hope that you are too and share in my joy.

When you think about the sheer pot-pourri of chance and circumstance that actually led to the creation of life on earth you have to be humbled. In truth, we would seem to the "happy accident" of all that could have happened.

Just the right elements, atoms and molecules fused together at just the right time, in exactly the right proportions, at just right place, with just the right amount of heat to bring together the happy chance that is us, mankind. And that happy set of circumstances created the air we breathe and the atmosphere we live in and it put life on earth.

Wow! With totally wide-eyed wonder, what else can you say?

Life truly is a miracle of chance and circumstance and by the law of degeneration that is built into our DNA, we wear out. Everything about us ultimately ages out and we are given a life expectancy of just *"three score years and ten"* ... that's 70 years, give or take.

Now I don't know about you, but I am determined not to waste any of it. Life is short enough as it as and I don't have time for excuses, or the dead weight of failure ... or failures. Sorry, but I don't.

I want to be a winner and I am determined to make you a winner too.

We all of us have the choice. We can make it work, or we can sit back and wonder why it didn't. And when I get to the grand old age of retirement, as one day you will too, I want to have lived a worthy, productive, successful and people-oriented life.

I want to look back on my life and enjoy it once again with the same incredulous wide-eyed wonder that it was the success I always wanted it to be. And I am determined to make it and turn it into that success by being true to myself, generous with my time, respectful of other people and focused on earning the success that I am convinced I deserve.

Doesn't that sound like a plan to you? Isn't that something you'd like to share in? Don't you have that ... the determination to succeed by enriching your own life and the lives of everyone that you come into contact with?

If that kind of life is for sale, then I for one am willing and ready to buy into it!

> *"A man who dares to waste one hour of time has not*
> *discovered the value of life."*
>
> Charles Darwin, 1809 - 1882

3. Courage

As the late soul singer Marvin Gaye once put it, *"It takes every kind of people to make the word go round."* Now, ain't that the truth!

There is no telling how any man or woman may act in a given set of circumstances. How few of us today, I wonder, could have shown the courage and defiance of the many, many soldiers who stood bravely in the trenches in World War One and exchanged fire with fellow human beings across a no man's land measuring not much more than a football pitch?

Could you have done that? I'm no coward, but I know that I could not and I salute those brave men and women that did. All of them are my heroes.

More than 9 million soldiers died on various battlefields in WW1. Nine million brave souls who died doing what most of us could not do.

But it takes all kinds of courage. Courage just to get through life. Courage to survive. Courage to make great and small things happen. Courage to face your own weaknesses and square up to the challenges that life continually presents.

How do you measure up? That's the question you have to ask yourself and it's the question that only you can answer.

It takes courage to start your own business. It takes courage to deal with failure. It takes courage to admit when you're wrong. In short, there are many types of courage that all help to shape the person you are.

But if you are to succeed in business the way you've planned and hope for, then you have to have courage. You have to confront your demons - whatever they are - and you must deal with and defeat them.

If you don't, those demons will come to control you. They will come to haunt you, stunt your growth and repeatedly diminish all of your achievements.

As Stephen Pierce puts it in his worthy book *Secrets to Creating Wealth*, *"What you cannot correct and what you are unwilling to confront is going to dominate your life. It will control you."*

Now that is right on the money. I have seen great minds with superb ideas, fail, fold and fumble in the face of challenge and pressure. They lacked to courage to confront their demons and make things work out.

Remember, whether you work for yourself, or you are someone else's wage slave, every day is a heap of problems. Every single day, without exception, you are going to be beset by a string of problems. You have to deal with them. You have to resolve them and find a solution that works. That's your job, Mr Problem-Solver! That is how great (and small!) things happen - because someone chose to fix it.

The problem is unlikely to go away. It might get shunted into someone else's in-tray, but it is not simply going to disappear. After all, this is the real world where grown ups fight and hassle, barter and haggle for their corner!

And small problems, if left unresolved, can quickly escalate into major issues. All because someone didn't grasp the situation, take control and wasn't brave enough to deal with the issues.

If you're the boss, that's your job - dealing with things. That's why you're the boss. You've got the initiative, the tools, the charm (I hope!) and the capability to *"keep your head when all about you are losing theirs"!* You can do it, often when others cannot. You analyse the issues, plan a solution and drive it through. Everybody's happy. Life, it can be so beautifully simple, can't it?

I'm a boss too and everyday, I face issues, hundreds of them. I resolve many if not most and some days I even get to resolve them all. And tomorrow? Well, there'll be hundreds more and the day after that too and every day after until I retire, or expire!

But I have a special trick that I'd like to share with you. Most of my days split into "nice" issues and "nasty" issues.

Nice issues are the things that make you happy when you've resolved them and you know that whatever else you have to do it will be a relatively pleasant experience.

Nasty issues are the problem phone calls that you have to make, or the dressing downs you have to give, or the rallying calls you're forced to make to the troops to improve bottom line performance. These are the ones that linger in your mind, the ones you can always find a thousand excuses not to deal with.

Guess what? These are the issues I deal with first, every single day that I ever sit down. Why? Because once they are out of the way, the "monkey that has been sitting on my shoulder" has totally disappeared. I'm free to make all of those pleasant calls and deal with those nice non-confrontational issues. Free to get on with the business of making money and working with my team of people.

And I've got the whole day ahead of me, without any "nasties" clouding my conscience and making it difficult for me to concentrate. My simple action turns my whole day into a pleasure and frees the "creative juices" to get flowing again, with no unpleasant irritations rumbling round in the back of my mind.

There you go, a different kind of courage, but it still takes courage to confront issues, problems and events and deal with them, positively. If you don't have that courage, those events can easily bring you and your business down.

Take courage in who you are and all that you can accomplish. Hold onto your beliefs and be strong.

You'll be glad you did in a million and more business situations, today and far into the future.

> *"Courage is going from failure to failure without losing enthusiasm."*
> Sir Winston Churchill

4. Conviction

If you don't believe in it, or believe in yourself and all that you are trying to do, how can you possibly expect anyone else to?

You've got belief, you've got determination and you've got courage, now all you need is at least a little (or preferably a lot!) of conviction.

In business, you want someone else to buy into your dreams. That is what you are trying to do - convince somebody they want what you have to sell. They might not need it, but that's an entirely different matter. People buy what they want, not what they need.

Let me give you an example. A close friend of mine is a bargain hunter clothes shopper. Every year he waits eagerly for the sales to come around, especially the big name label brands such as Armani, Hugo Boss, Ralph Lauren, Dunhill, and Ermenegildo Zegna.

One year, we pitched up at his favourite shop and there was a full-length leather coat in soft black nappa leather. It was substantially reduced and was being offered at 40% of its original asking price, which was a few thousand pounds.

When he first saw it, my friend's eyes spun with delight and desire. I knew he would have to have this coat. I watched him drool over the coat and he confessed that while he didn't need it, he so much wanted it! He hummed and hawed and ha'd and I watched as the shop staff wasted their lives waiting for him to make up his mind about the purchase.

After some deliberation, he bought the coat, much to everyone's relief. Outside it was raining hard, but he didn't want to wear his new coat because "it would get wet"! It was a rain-proofed overcoat that he had just bought!

As we made our way to the crowded car park, doubt began to creep in. He began the process of deliberation and justification. Could he afford it? Would it enhance his wardrobe? Did it work with everything else he had?

By the time we reached the car, he had almost talked

Live **BIG**. Think **LARGE**. Act **SENSIBLY**.
How to make a fortune - without losing your friends!

himself out of the purchase and into taking the item back to the shop for a refund (highly unlikely!). It was left to me to point out to him that he had all but destroyed the pleasure of the purchase he had made. Now, when he wore it, instead of delighting in his purchase and being the proud owner of such a beautiful new coat, he was riddled with doubt about the "sense of his purchase".

He had totally lost conviction in what he had done and soured the experience in ways that would make it hard to retrieve that first flush of satisfaction in a "job well done".

Ever done that yourself? Bought something and then wished you hadn't. We all have!

But the point I am making is that in business if you want to be super successful you must move forward with total conviction. There isn't much room for doubt and wavering. You've done the research (hopefully!). You've modelled and remodelled your decisions and then re-evaluated the pathway that led you act in the way you are going to. Don't let courage fail you now!

Keep the strength of your convictions. Believe in yourself. Dismiss the doubters and destroy the whispers in your head. You've reached the decision you've made for all of the right reasons and you must have the conviction to carry it through.

After all, if you don't believe in it how can you expect others to?

Sure, there's a possibility you'll fail. There is always is and in life nothing is ever certain except, as the old line tells us - death and taxes! (And, I believe, uncertainty!)

The important thing is that whatever it is, you see it through and hold fast to your beliefs and conviction.

Think no one has ever failed? Colonel Sanders of Kentucky Fried Chicken fame whose outlets you now see everywhere started out flat broke with just his chicken recipe. Two thousand (yes, 2,000!) restaurants turned him down in his bid to get started. Wonder who's laughing now?

Walt Disney, the great man himself was no stranger to failure. On the way to the top he was declared bankrupt, but today the empire that bears his name has an operating income in excess of $3 billion per annum.

Me, I'm no stranger to failure either. I once printed 10,000 reply cards to a mailshot I was running with nowhere for anyone to write their name and address details anywhere on the card but I did remember to include the reply address!

I've also lost money making the wrong type of offers to untested lists of potential customers and once I put the wrong links into an email broadcast! I've only just recently started accepting Paypal payments and I wonder how much revenue I've lost because I didn't always make it easy enough for customers to pay me in as many ways that they could.

Clever me. Needless to say, I have never repeated those silly kind of mistakes since.

Failure isn't the problem. On its own, it never is - it's how you deal with it that matters. How you work to put it right, how you regroup, rebuild and reassemble to challenge the front line, once more. It's very simple, really, you can curl up and disappear, or you can pick yourself, dust yourself off, start all over again and give it your very best shot. But this time you'll be a lot smarter, a little wiser and much more capable. Failure teaches you those lessons.

Hey, if business was easy, everybody would be doing it! Look around you. They're not. Doesn't that tell you something?

"You must stick to your conviction, but be ready to abandon your assumptions."

Denis Waitley, internationally renowned business speaker

5. Humility

It takes a brave man or woman to admit it when they're wrong, but it takes a fool to keep going when they are!

There's nothing worse in any company than someone that believes they know everything and that they have nothing left to learn. There isn't a millionaire, multimillionaire, billionaire, or successful businessperson that I've ever met that didn't impress me with the depth and scale of their knowledge ... and their ability to listen and learn even more!

Successful people are like huge sponges. Their brain is no bigger than yours or mine, it's true, but what they can do with theirs is often astonishing! They soak up everything. They're onto every new wave in an instant. They're informed, aware and receptive. They listen keenly, often intently, to what 'people that count' have to say. They want to know. They are eager and hungry for information because they know that when they feed their minds, they open the gateway to opportunity.

E M Forster summed it up neatly in his stodgy bestselling book (don't bother - you'll die of boredom!) *Howard's End* with this one statement *"Only connect."* Everything else apart, he was spot on ... business, life, science, social relationships, intelligence - to succeed you simply have to make "the right connections".

And the whole of history is littered with people who have made all of "the right connections".

IBM had the machine, Bill Gates had the software, but it was Gates who made all of "the right connections" and created the immensely successful global monstrosity that Microsoft has become. And where does IBM now sit on the world's map of global influence?

Alta Vista, Excite and Yahoo had the ideas, they already had the market and saw the possibilities, but it was Larry Page & Sergei Brin that made all of "the right connections" and catapulted Google into the world's consciousness. Google is more than just a search engine, it's a way of life that has altered the way everyone does business and changed how the world now thinks, learns, listens and links.

Tim Berners Lee might have created the World Wide Web back in 1989, but a lot of other people have gone on to make even better connections from it, because of it and through it, making them immensely rich in the process simply by making "the right connections".

You see what I'm saying here? The idea is one thing and it is a very valuable thing in its own right, even a wonderful thing, but an idea on its own won't take you very far ... unless you can make all of "the right connections".

It's the dumb blonde defence ... " Connections created the constellations for the ancient Greeks. Look at the sky at night and all you'll see are random stars, but if you know how to make the right connections you can actually see 88 mythological-based star patterns."

Only connect … that's how markets are started and that's where success begins.

You see how everything works? It's these subtle interplays, these interlinked connections that make everything work. What has E M Forster got to do with your success? Everything and nothing. If you can't see the connection after all that I've said, then I can't help you. No one can. But if you get it, you've got one of the really big numbers in the combination that unlocks the door to your success.

In my own short life, I've met too many people that have been too full of their own self-importance. Too many people who are all too eager to tell you what their point of view is and why you should buy into it and trade off it. Too many people who simply forget to do you the courtesy of listening to what your point of view is and tuning in to what you have to say. Don't you find that it's hard to see when you're eyes are closed?

It doesn't take much to make everyone feel important. A quiet word here, a compliment there, a reward, an award, a simple kindness and suddenly you've made someone stand straighter, walk taller and work harder. Imagine if you did that for 20 people, or 50, 100, 500 or thousands. What do you think the effect on output, performance, profit and delivery might be?

It makes me buzz just thinking about it. Instead of a culture of monotonous drudgery, you create a culture of inspired harmony. People get in to work earlier because they want to, not because they have to. There's a cheerful buzz in every department and on every floor. They leave later without expecting overtime payment. Cheques are thudding in and the performance graph line is shooting off the scale. The business has never been healthier, more under control, or more capable and the future has never been brighter.

Sounds like Never, Never Land? It shouldn't. I've seen it happen and I've heard it expounded as more than a theory at many workshops I've been to all around the world.

You're the boss. You make great things happen … or you don't. Since failure to quote the well-polished cliché is not an option, it's up to you to do everything you possibly can to create success. That means making "the right connections", in just the right order and in just the right amounts to create, foster and sustain success.

And yes, it means a little humility too, if you are to make truly great things happen in your life. Making "the right connections" means it isn't just about you. It's about others too. You can't do it alone and you need to respect the people that help to make great things happen for you.

In my experience, too few bosses seem to grasp this simple principle. They have a penny-pinching attitude in everything they do which rebounds on everyone they deal with.

They nail their suppliers to the tightest possible margin. They pay the meanest lowest wages they can get away with. They haggle over quality, always looking ways to "knock a bit more off".

Everyone suffers while they drive big, flashy cars, have lavishly furnished offices, take months off at a time to recharge themselves in their exotic holiday homes. Everyone else does the work, but no one else gets the gravy. It's a business going nowhere, built on stilts and balanced on sand. Everyone hates it and wants to leave. No one is inspired or enthusiastic and the management is a constant topic of scorn, undisguised hatred and derision.

For want of just a little humility all of the business's natural goodness is being destroyed, eaten away. We all recognise it because at some time or another, we've all worked there. We've seen that same boss, experienced that same unhappiness and swore that one day, some day, we'd do it better.

Have we? Did we? Can we?

A bad boss, a tyrant, or a bully doesn't realise that he or she is actually diminishing their own stature in everything they do. They're thinking small, but acting big. They're stooping down when they should be standing up. They're acting idiotically leaving goodwill on the floor, money on the table and letting ideas fly out of the window.

Remember the title of this book? Let me remind you, it is, **Live BIG. Think LARGE. Act SENSIBLY.** Be the person you want to become, understand the value of connections, practice the art of humility and you hold in your hands half of the combination to the door of rampant personal success.

Be mindful of and always try to live up to the expectations of others and remember to reward their expectations of you.

"Pride makes us artificial, humility makes us real"
Thomas Merton, Trappist Monk, 1915-1968

▬▬▬▬▬▬▬ *6. A rapacious need for knowledge - and results!*

Most of the successful people I know and have met have this essential quality in abundance. *They simply need to know!* About everything! When something strikes them, they won't rest until they find the answer, or some sort of answer. That's a big part of what makes them successful - the quest for knowledge, the hunger to learn and the need to know.

Information is knowledge, answers are knowledge and knowledge brings about results.

Don't believe me? What's the best day to send out your electronic direct mail, or your e-newsletter? How is an advert actually read and tracked by the eye? How is this different from the way a search engine web page gets viewed? Which is going to work best … an envelope that features a handwritten address, has no return address on it and has a colourful stamp stuck in the corner, or an envelope, with a see-through window, a printed return address and a big black postal mark slapped somewhere in the top corner?

Okay, the last one was a dead giveaway, but this is all common knowledge … *if you know where to look.* And if you are to succeed in business, you simply do have to know where to look. That's what makes Google such a friend and ally. If you want it, want to know it and it exists, then it is likely that it is sitting somewhere on Google. Just type in what it is that you're looking for and, hey presto, there it is and with enough options to keep you happy for years.

In business, it's often knowledge that keeps us alive. Hey, I'm serious, so please listen up! It's knowledge and awareness that stop you from making big mistakes ... like trying to sell a product that's already well past its sell-by date.

Markets move in waves. One minute, they're hot and the next they're not. Who would now attempt to make their fortune moving 3.5" floppy disks? And VCRs are as cheap as chips. No one wants them any more. Still, it's easy to get caught out with a product you can't move simply because you bought into someone's else's dream or, more likely, their past success.

I do see a lot of that. People getting caught up in the power of a wave that's already gone. Its force has been expended and the market can't carry anyone's dreams anymore. It's a tough thing to say, I guess, but a little more awareness and a lot more savvy would have saved a lot of heartache, much trouble and such awful distress. But then again, everyone has to start somewhere and the value of a lesson is never wasted on people that are ready to hear the answers.

So where do you look for knowledge? Read the press, the highbrow papers and the broadsheets too. There's usually something there that will spark the germ of an idea, reinforce what you're thinking or give you a whole new direction to look at. What are the trends? What are people buying, buying into and watching on TV?

People are fascinated by real life experiences and the programme *Who's Been Framed?* remains prime time television viewing. There's a business right there - showing people how to use their camcorder to produce films and DVDs that capture every moment perfectly!

Identity Fraud is a massive industry that is growing by millions year after year. Every day it features in practically every newspaper. There's a raft of businesses you can build right there in advising people how to stay safe and protect themselves from ID theft, on and offline.

And that's how it works - knowledge is information = opportunity + only connect! Make the right connections and that's how you make money and write your own success story.

Got a passion? Theatre, film, ballet, collecting, investing - whatever it is - just follow the shoals because that's where the big ideas are. What is motivating, concerning, angering, inspiring and moving all of the people that are interested in the same things that you are interested in? Read the online discussion forums. Look at and analyse the topics that have earned the most coverage because that's where the opportunities are and they are waiting for you!

Only connect. You see how these things are interlinked and keep on coming around?

A friend of mine's first venture into the software business came about because he could not keep an orderly track of all of the websites that he was visiting for answers, information and knowledge. It was frustrating him because time was being wasted simply recovering his tracks and time is the most precious resource that any of us has.

My friend wanted instant answers, but none existed. At the time, there wasn't software that he could load to manage his internet surfing activity. What did he do? He posted an advert for a software programmer, a webmaster, to write some. He told the programmer what he wanted and the webmaster wrote the program, trialling and testing it and refining it until it worked.

Then, when it was ready, my friend packaged it and sold it online. It has since proved to be a runaway bestseller that clearly filled a need and has provided the answer to the same sort of problems that other online users were experiencing. It has also netted my friend handsome profits ... for just a little bit of work and simply for making all of the right connections!

But results matter. And that's why I love the direct response industry, or direct marketing. You can see in an instant just what has happened with your idea and what you are offering. You can see your winners and your failures and you have the evidence to prove it, onscreen, right before your eyes.

It's much harder to track a TV commercial, a press advert or a burst of radio marketing. With those forms of messaging, you don't know exactly who you are reaching and you can't definitively say what happened. But you can waste an awful lot of money trying to find out! A lot of very big companies, worldwide, work this way. They have no real idea about what they are doing (and sometimes even why!) but they blindly continue because "that's the way it has always been done".

If you don't know the value of every advertising pound, dollar, yen, euro, or cent that you're spending ... then why are you doing it?

Surely, it makes sense for these companies to change their business model and refine their practices to get some sort of accountability into their business plan? And the internet has very much made this possible. You can test products, services, solutions, applications and offerings cheaper and more cost-effectively than at any time in history. And best of all, you can see exactly what happened and what the results were.

That essential information shapes your progress and

defines all of your next moves. And it can be uncovered very cheaply, without the need to spend millions in research trials, consumer tests and all of the other pre-market procedures that soak up vital revenue.

So, before you waste another nickel or penny on things that don't work, think about how you can make them work and how you can use resources that are readily available to find answers *and get results!*

Do everything you can to "feed your mind". You owe it to yourself to stretch yourself every day and if you really want to be successful, the more you know and can bring to the table - any table - the better your chances of success are going to be.

Do crossword puzzles and brainteasers that challenge your mind. Take tests, sit exams, write papers and do research about the things that interest you. Challenge yourself. Test and tax your memory. Make it better than it was yesterday and sharpen your skills so that even as you grow older and your skills start to wane you have developed a lifelong love of learning and a "need to know" hunger that will always drive you forward, no matter what age you reach.

Don't ever allow yourself to grow old! Too many people do that and hide behind the feeble excuse that "I'm 50, or 60, or 70 and what am I supposed to know?" Not acceptable, not if you want to be successful. Keep an open mind, travel with your eyes wide open, be receptive to change, understand trends and you will have opened your whole life to earn considerable capital rewards with the added bonuses of immense satisfaction, challenging commitment and great joy!

If your mind is young enough to cope, you will simply never grow old.

"We must learn our limits. We are all something, but none of us are everything."
Blaise Pascal, French mathematician, 1623-1662

"Knowing is not enough; we must apply. Willing is not enough; we must do."
Goethe, German Poet & Novelist. 1749-1832

7. The ability to completely "empty your cup"

It's a fool that thinks they have nothing left to learn and it's an idiot that feels they are too old to learn anything new. Embarrassment is a personal inadequacy that is very much like the fear of failure. Most of us won't because we are afraid of the consequences, afraid of looking (and feeling) foolish. So we don't.

Don't what? Ask out the best-looking girl we've ever seen! Try a new skill, or stand up to speak in public, even when we've got lots to say worth hearing! Don't take a chance on our own initiative with a business opportunity that looks very much like it will work. Then we curse ourselves when someone else steals in does what "we could so easily have done"! But didn't.

You know, it's all about letting go, but our stupid pride and our over-inflated sense of self-worth stop us from "seizing the moment". And you know what? That moment rarely, if ever, comes around again.

Remember when you first learned to swim? You were probably a young child, embarrassed about your body and full of self-consciousness. You were also afraid! The pool was big, noisy and more revolting than anything you'd ever smelled before. Everybody was much bigger than you. Water went in your eyes, up your nose and in your ears. Your head went under and you came up splashing, thrashing and coughing with panic and the sheer terror of it all! You clung to the side desperately afraid that if you let go you'd drown.

You watched people. You built up the courage. You wanted what they had and clearly enjoyed - the skill to swim and enjoy yourself in the water. Eventually you reached the point of now or never, do or die - you had to have a go. You had weighed up the odds, evaluated the situation and you were ready to give it a shot. Suddenly you were trying, even swimming a little. It sure wasn't pretty and the style marks were drastic but you were making progress sledging across the top of the water, arms thrashing, legs pumping and you were doing it … all by yourself.

A fear was conquered and a valuable skill was learned. No more arm bands, floats and rubber rings. No more nights of anxious fear before you were dragged reluctantly to the swimming pool. You were now a swimmer and, "Hey girls, look at me!" was suddenly your new way of looking at the world. Made a difference to your life and the way you now saw yourself, didn't it?

And why not? Swimming is such a valuable skill, often learned the hard way, just like riding a bike. Now why not apply that same logic to your adult life? Think about the steps you went through to learn swimming, one of life's most important self-preservation skills. What has changed? You're a little bit older, perhaps a lot wiser, but you still have to wrap your head around many different challenges every single day.

Get into the habit of getting off your high horse. If you don't know how to do something, don't ever be afraid to ask. It will save you hours of frustration as you try to learn or try to find out what somebody can show you in a matter of seconds.

Case in point. I love to work in Microsoft Word but the program can be so frustrating, especially if you are trying to edit a document that someone else has already formatted. Working against the pressure of time, I was trying to do a simple fix on a file.

All I wanted to do was remove unsightly spaces, but try as I might, there was no way that I could uncover the answer. The Help menu didn't! The program instructions offered no advice. Having searched online for an answer that I just couldn't find and wasted 50 minutes or more of my own valuable life, I finally called a Word expert that I knew. He showed me how to do what I had struggled so hard to do for almost an hour in less than ten seconds!

But then again, I have never been afraid to completely empty my cup. There are people who know more than I ever will. There are people who are more skilled at the things I do and want to be good at it. There are people that I meet in business who are considerably younger than me and who are probably twice as sharp. And I'm glad about it!

I feed off them and I learn from them. I reassess who I am, what I want and where I am going every time I encounter them and always I believe that I am better by far for the experience of being challenged by them.

It's the same with unfamiliar situations in life and in business that take me outside of my own comfort zone. I relish the challenge and welcome the opportunity and I urge you to do the same.

Sure, it has something to do with regret. When I was a young man the girl that stole my heart was a picture! I was totally besmitten by her and followed her practically everywhere. She never knew and I never believed that someone as ordinary as I was, someone with my hopeless inadequacies (remember I had barely learned to swim!) could ever capture such a glittering prize. So I never asked her out. I could never empty my cup enough to put myself in the hands of someone who could shape the next few days, months, weeks, even years, or possibly the whole of my life! Couldn't face the possibility of a rejection, or put down, so I never tried to open the door. Fear meant I couldn't let go, when I most needed to.

It was many years later in my adult life that I bumped quite by accident and in a different part of the country into the woman who first stole my heart. By this time I had settled down with my long term girl friend, bought a house and were expecting our 1st child. We chatted about our lives and our career paths and she invited me to lunch. All went well until under the influence of a blazing log fire and a little too much wine she told me she had a personal confession to make that she'd very much like me to hear.

I knew what was coming and I have regretted it ever since. She told me, without any embarrassment, that she had been crazy about me for years while we were at school, but had always assumed that I wasn't interested because despite her giving me repeated signals I had never asked her out! Under the sweet pain of protest, I never knew. I had never read the signals and, possibly, one of the greatest opportunities of my life had sailed on sweetly by. Wherever you are, Maria, and if you should ever get to read this book, you still have a part of my heart! Please keep it safe.

Some time later, after I had read Joe Hyams book, I started self-defence classes in martial arts. I was in my early twenties at the time and began as all students do at the very bottom of the ladder, a white belt. It was both a humbling and uplifting experience. There I was, not the oldest, nor the youngest student in the dojo (classroom), but one with the most to learn.

At times, it was excruciating to be so incompetent, but it was always rewarding. Working in such close contact with people who were seriously skilled in the art of "offensive self defence" I learned much about the human psyche and myself. I had to completely empty my cup and rid myself of all airs and pretences. Successful businessman I might have been outside the dojo, but once inside I was simply another student. It was awe-inspiring and I laboured to learn, but the rewards were immense.

Now, I walk into strange places and I am no longer afraid. I know how to quickly get into position to defend myself. I know how to present the smallest possible target to an opponent and how to use techniques that give me an "offensive measure of self defence and control". And that's the thing - I am better able to control my response to the flight-or-fight reflex and I am aware of all that is going around me, ready and able to respond to dangerous situations. That alone provides an awesome amount of self-confidence and belief.

I learnt once again how people learn and I conquered the terrifying fear of letting go of the handrail at the poolside. I was made to feel small and exposed by my own inadequacies, but I was enriched by the experiences that I had.

You too have to let go. You have to conquer your demons, face your fears, come to terms with who you are and "build a better you", day by day, thought by thought, experience by experience.

It's called life and far too many people don't actually live it … they simply let their lives roll by as they try to live out their dreams in other people's successes. To me, you're just using the wrong end of the telescope.

If this life is all you'll ever have, don't you owe it to yourself to do something worthwhile with it? Isn't it time you became the person you want to become? Or at least gave it a shot …?

> *"Experience is the best teacher, but a fool will learn from no one."*
> Benjamin Franklin, American Statesman, 1706-1790

> *"It's the heart afraid of breaking that never learns to dance. It is the dream afraid of waking that never takes the chance. It is the one who won't be taken who cannot seem to give. And the soul afraid of dying that never learns to live."*
> Bette Midler, American Singer & Actress

8. A plan

It's one thing to talk about it and it's a totally different thing to actually do it. Talk will get you everywhere, but if all you ever do is talk then the reality will take you precisely nowhere. In my life, probably like yours, I've met a lot of good talkers.

They paint wonderful pictures with their words. They build huge mansions with sweeping staircases, enormous gardens, grand views, lavish rooms and all of it echoes with the cavernous and resounding hollowness of emptiness. *Yes, we're going right back to Sidcup!*

It's true that talk is cheap and it costs you absolutely nothing. But it's also armour that too many businesspeople and would-be wanna-be's wear all too readily. It is their shield and it becomes their excuse for simply "not doing". *If I could only get to Sidcup…*

Barbara Sher, American motivational self-help counsellor and bestseling author, put it beautifully when she said: *"I could do anything, if only I knew what it was!"*

We fail, so often, simply because we fail to plan often enough! Success really is and can be that simple.

So, where does it begin? It begins with a plan. It begins with an idea of where it is that you want to go, but first of all you've got to buy a ticket and get on the train. And to do that, you need to know where you're going and where you want to end up. Everything starts with a dream, but it is the plan that will take you there.

I've often been asked the same question at functions, dinner parties and business events and it goes something this: *"Don't we all have a plan that we're given from Day One?"* What these people are saying is that our lives are pretty much mapped out before we even take our first breath!

Have you any idea how daft that sounds? Weigh up the evidence of your own life and the lives of others too. The idea that we're all working to some grand scheme, some predestined range of success and failure is simply ridiculous. If you think I'm being brutal here, you must forgive me, but as I see it, this is the truth as I have experienced it.

I've met the kid from the Bronx who was born the wrong side of the line but who grew up to be a phenomenal success. In many ways, we all have because these people are all around us. There is no predetermined right to success and failure! That outcome of your life is entirely in your own hands and that is the beauty of the life we are all living … we actually get to choose! All of us, we get to choose and choice is a powerful thing. It makes heroes and it makes beggars, it makes clowns and princes and it turns dreamers into legends, like John Lennon, Freddie Mercury and Marilyn Monroe. Their tragedies turned them into legends, but their choices made them everyday heroes.

"If only I could be like that … " You can, but it won't be easy. It wasn't for them and they made huge sacrifices, some bad career choices and were influenced by some lousy advisors, but they had a dream and came up with a plan that worked.

Most people in life and many people in business settle for whatever comes along. They say they're happy to keep their head down below the parapet where they can't be seen. Happy to be bypassed and overlooked when the top jobs are on offer. Happy to be part of the formless grey mass that is the rank and file of many companies. But they're not happy. Not really. They're living a lie and they're telling everyone who'll listen that same old lie. How sad is that?

If you want something better, you've got to plan how you are going to get it because it "won't just happen". Success rarely ever does and when the opportunity presents itself, you've got to seize the moment.

It might not be your own plan that you'll use to gain momentum, get lift off and shape the success of your own future. There are a lot of successful business people who have used other people's plans to realise their dreams and ambitions. Go to business seminars, get online and do your homework. Find out who these people are and how you can get hold of their plans. If the plan has worked successfully for them, why can't it work as successfully for you?

I've done it and from time to time I still do. I buy other people's plans and reshape them into delivering my own dreams. I've bought licenses to products that other people have created and made considerable sums of money by repackaging the products and also by selling licenses of the same product to other people. That's why I believe it is important that you make all the right connections. It's a sure way to make good money easily by genuinely providing something that everybody wants.

Tell me this, how do you plan your day? If you don't, you should. If you do, you should look at ways in which you can improve the way your time is used. I'm reminded here of a quotation that I've carried with me since I was a small boy and it's this: *"If it wasn't for the small things, I could achieve great things!"*

There's a stone of truth in there and it affects us all. We allow small, peripheral and incidental things to infiltrate our lives and they subtract substantially from the quality of our achievements. How much time did you waste today? Reading the paper, chattering idly, discussing irrelevant and totally trivial things and letting things that don't really matter slow you down and impair your vision.

Successful people don't do that. Most are mean timekeepers, who can be hard on themselves and expectant of others. That's what made them successful and that's what success is about - shaping and defining the dream and planning the detail that will lead to its ultimate capture and eventual realisation. It's all in the planning.

But success needn't be a military-styled operation. There's nothing worse in anyone's life than stifling regimentation. It's a straitjacket that can drive you mad. You plan has to be flexible enough to accommodate change, as it happens. That is the one constant in life - everything changes and pretty much all of the time!

You have to know how to master change and make it work for you. That, as much as anything, is exactly what success is all about - recognising changing patterns and be able to move with them.

Think what has changed over just the past 10 years. Flat screen TVs, flatscreen PC monitors, in-car navigation systems, the iPOD, notebooks that are quicker, better equipped and more capable than your lumbering desktop PC, mobile phones with internet connectivity, voice calls over your PC, email and Google - to name just a handful.

You couldn't plan for much of that to happen unless you really had insider knowledge, but if your plan for success was adaptable enough and had flexibility built in you could have made more than one tidy fortune just from changing track in midstream. And I'll bet lots of smart entrepreneurs did too.

The point is that your plan is never cast in stone. It should be a "loosely flexible framework" that gives you points of reference to work toward and surfaces from which you can feed off and push off into other areas and new dimensions. Your plan gives you the fuel you need as Star Trek bravely puts it to: *"Boldly go!"*

Regimentation rarely works. Life just isn't made that way. You need a general idea of where you are going and what you are trying to achieve and accomplish, but it would be a very rare thing if you ever got there without both major and minor changes to your plan along the way.

I have a friend who set himself the target twelve years ago of "saving himself rich". Yes, he was paid quite handsomely for what he did and the plan was that he would save pretty much most of what he earned so that, by the time he was 50, some 20 years away, he would have a nice tidy pile. But as you can probably guess, life got in the way. He was hit by a costly divorce, lost his well-paid job, struggled through three different careers and, the last time I saw him, he was looking for another job and struggling … without a plan.

While you can't map out the future, you can put down some very important markers that will guide you toward the future that you want to see. You've got to start out with some idea of where you are going. That's what I call a plan.

"If you are going to achieve excellence in big things, you develop the habit in little matters. Excellence is not an exception, it is a prevailing attitude."
Colin Powell, former US Secretary of State

"If you don't have a plan for yourself, you'll almost certainly be part of someone else's!"
American Proverb

9. A dream

In Baz Luhrman's genre redefining movie masterpiece of Shakespeare's romantic tragedy Romeo & Juliet, there's a song that says: *"I had a dream last night, and it fit me like a glove."*

Active minds dream every night and apparently it's a good thing that we do. Dreams it seems help us to keep a grasp on our own reality. In dreams we live out the things that scare us, drive us and concern us in our daily lives. Asleep in dreamland, we can all be heroes and abject failures, rampant successes and awkwardly clumsy contributors all in the same evening!

Dreams give us goals. They fuel our ambition and provide the passion that drives us to succeed. You can see it. You know you want it. The only question that remains to be answered is how you are going to get whatever it is that you so passionately want.

To be honest, I didn't start out with dreams that were any different to your own. Sure, I wanted to be successful. I wanted a nice home, a wonderful family, freedom from debt and enough money to be able to do whatever I chose, whenever I chose and as often as I would like to. I also wanted to be able to retire early. No, really early, like 40 say, or 45 and not to have to work any more. Ever, unless I wanted to.

Oh and I would have loved to have been honoured by my country and "capped" just once, for anything! Could have been rounders - I would not have minded, but of course it never happened and as I've grown older I've come to accept that doors close quickly behind you. You've probably had the doors shut on a few of your own dreams already … rock star, champion cyclist, professional footballer, CEO of a Fortune 500 company and, no doubt, several others too.

But what's happened as the years have flown doesn't and hasn't ever stopped me dreaming. I'm still passionate about my dreams and the things I have to do with the rest of my life.

However, as young man, I was invited to a "financial presentation" in the City of London. Basically, a whiz with personal finance was about to "sort out my life" and put me on a path that would enable me to realise my dreams. (Savings, pensions and some other minor investments, no doubt. Isn't it funny how they always keep the cream of the investments, the mega-earners, for themselves?)

Reluctantly, I sat before this sharp suited, eager eagle who had been recommended to me by a personal friend. Out came his clearly obscenely expensive fountain pen and with a theatrical flourish he laid the paper that would plot the very path to the destination of my dreams before him on the desk.

And so we began with typical questions about the current state of my financial health and how I saw things developing in the future. Then we got to the nuts and bolts about what I wanted to achieve. How was I to measure the success that he was about to set up for me? And that's when it all started to fall apart!

Did I want a swimming pool? No. Did I want a country mansion with many bedrooms? No. Did I want to own a yacht? No. Did I want racehorses? No. Did I want a tennis court? No. Did I want to own holiday homes abroad? No. This went on for quite some time and I could see the sharp young professional gentleman sitting before me growing increasingly frustrated by my non-committal answers. Finally he looked up and fixed his eyes on me. With an exasperated air he said: *Mr James, I am going to write down that you have a 'Poverty of Ambition'. Is that okay with you?"*

I have never forgotten that moment. You see, in the example I've given you, you are not defining dreams, you are defining desires and there is a whole world of difference.

Desires such as those listed above are simply objects of immediate gratification. You want it, you get it, you forget all about it. Remember the bike you wanted when you were young? You got it and you rode it proudly, oh, for at least a week. You lovingly cared for it for at least a few days. Then you promptly forgot all about it, forgot to clean it, forgot even to ride it and when it became shabby you gave it away. That wasn't a dream, it was simply the desire of ownership and, once the desire for ownership has been satisfied, everything changes.

Just think about the things you've wanted and what happened to them after you got them. The wonderful surround sound system you've got, your expensive car, the flatscreen TV, your sit-on lawnmower, the Cartier watch - everything that once was an object of desire, a "must-have" is superseded almost immediately by the next object of desire in a never-ending chase for ownership that will never ever be satisfied. There will always be something else that you want. That's how life is.

Dreams are different. They are not objects of instant gratification, things that can be tossed aside easily as soon as they have been reached. Conquering Mount Everest would be a dream for most people and certainly not something that you would ever toss aside lightly after you had succeeded.

However, owning your dream car, a Lamborghini, Ferrari, Porsche or McClaren, is probably something you would put aside, once the desire for ownership has been finally satisfied. It's just the way life is. One "desire" is checked off and quickly replaced by the next item on your "desire list".

But aren't dreams and desires one and the same thing for most people? That's the confusion and no, they're not.

The dictionary makes the differentiation a little clearer. Here's what it says:

Dream: cherished aspiration, ambition or ideal.

Desire: to strongly wish for or want something.

A desire is something you want and that demands instant gratification - a purchase, for example, as we've already shown in the examples I've given you.

But a dream is what gets you out of bed every day. A desire might, but it is unlikely to fuel your longterm ambitions ... those are bound up with your dreams.

Stuart Goldsmith in his book *Seven Secrets of the Millionaires* writes that he believes that everything starts with a dream. You've got to be sure about what it is that you want a year from now, a month from now, a week from now and right now and then set about earning and achieving your dreams. He offers five valuable tips to help you structure your thinking:

1. Dream about what it is that you want
2. Be realistic about you want
3. Do something about getting what you want
4. Be focused & disciplined in your approach
5. Start now!

These are the five tips that Stuart strongly believes can guide you - as they have guided him - to achieve enormous independent wealth.

I'd simply like to add that you shouldn't confuse your dreams with your desires.

My dream? Not much has changed for me. I still want to be successful with all of my businesses, which should mean that I will be profitable and earn more than enough money to finance all of my desires. Now, I wouldn't call that a *Poverty of Ambition* would you?

Set your mind on the target of becoming the best in your field of business. Don't concentrate on the money. Life isn't just about the money. In fact, my father questioned me about this recently. He was "questioning" my goals and my targets, my aims and ambitions. He thought (wrongly) that I was being materialistic, but as I explained to him, money is only part of the equation. Money buys you a better life. It frees you from constant worry. It gives you freedom from the daily drudgery that being a wage slave can often be. It allows you to explore and pursue other interests and it enables you to become the person you want to be. That is the power of money and that is what it can do for you.

You should never underestimate the power of money and all that it can do and, if your dream is success, then all of your desires will be answered by the successes you create and continue to create.

But everything that can ever be and all that you can ever become starts with your own dreams of success. Dream of simply being the best businessperson you can be running the most successful businesses you could ever run and that will create all of the success you deserve.

A dream is your ticket to travel, anywhere that you want to go. A desire is just a signpost along the way. And money is just a means to an end. Money is the fuel that enables you to do anything that you want to do and it allows you to live your life entirely on your own terms ... dependent on no one but yourself and without anyone else's interference. Now that's my kind of life!

> *"The only thing that will stop you from fulfilling your dreams is you."*
> Tom Bradley, American politician & baseball player

10. A destination

So, you've got the first nine essential elements to success firmly in your locker. You're on your way ... but where are you going? What is your final destination and will you recognise it when you arrive?

When is enough ever enough? When have you really made it and truly arrived? Is there ever an ultimate destination? And will your destination be like the end of the rainbow? You can see it but it is always somehow just out of reach.

You've got to start out by knowing where you are going because nothing good, worthwhile or lasting is likely to happen by chance. Look at your life to this point. "It", the great thing you desire hasn't ever happened by chance so far, has it? Great things happen because you make them and there's no witch's brew or magic potion that I know of that can help you to do that.

Stephen Pierce, in his book, *Secrets to Creating Wealth*,

said it best with his observation: *"Successful people make decisions that create the future they desire. Unsuccessful people make decisions that create the present they deserve."* Everyone has a choice.

Far too many people, as I've already said, take the attitude, *"Oh, I can't deal with that day!"* Or any other day, come to that. They never make those decisions that will lead them to the destination of their dreams because they never will. It's just too hard and they don't really want to. They talk like they do, but inside I suspect that they know they never will. *So once again it's back to Sidcup!*

You've got to start out with some idea of where it is that you're going. What is it that, ultimately, you want to achieve? Early retirement, a bigger house, a few houses, holiday homes in far-away places, land, capital, reputation, resource - whatever your dream, that's your destination. You put a price on it and you give it its value. They are your shares, shares in your dreams and you can give them to whoever you want, or you can keep them all to yourself. You get to choose and one of the most persistent themes throughout my book is the power of choice. And what a wonderful thing it is!

Exercised properly, choice is an immensely powerful tool. It shapes you and your dreams. It adds value to your life, provides reasons for actions and makes sense out of much of what you do.

Personally, I have chosen my destinations as carefully as anyone could have. I don't really want the "badges of show and the labels of wealth". Many houses, lots of cars, ships, boats, planes and racing cars have never really inspired me. One day, maybe they will, but right now I just want to continue being good at what I do, crafting excellence in all of my businesses and making sure that I deliver on every promise that I ever make - to myself and to everyone else.

Sounds corny and too good to be true? I can assure you that it isn't. I got past the "envy" stage a long, long time ago. When you've made enough money so that money doesn't really matter any more, I can tell you that it changes your perspective and alters your thinking.

And one of the best destinations that I have ever reached was becoming "wholly and entirely debt-free". Now that is a great way to live your life. When you finally get to that destination, you'll know that a great weight has been lifted. The thunderclouds have finally rolled away and you are free and, boy, does it feel good! You can pay for anything you want and whatever you need, any time you choose, whenever and just as often as it suits you. What a great way to live your life!

But what about your own destination? What do you want from the life you're leading, or what is it that life is not giving you right now?

You want health? Well, that's a good destination and, yes, you can earn it! Start today. Go out and buy yourself a bike, a mountain bike or racing cycle, it doesn't matter which. Set yourself a programme, get on it and ride your way to better health - and, yes, it can be that easy! Join a gym or local health club and, even if you look like Miss Piggy or Homer Simpson, get your kit on, get down there and get after your dream of a new, fitter looking, slender you. It's a great destination and practically everyone can get there at some level of another. Lose the fear. No one's laughing at you because frankly no one's that interested in you.

It's a weird thing how we all believe that "everyone will be looking" at us. How can we suddenly become the centre of everyone's universe? Others may give us a glance, but that's about it. It's more likely that we "don't register" and they've moved on while we still think (mistakenly) that they are concentrating on our shape and somewhat pathetic range of skills. Sorry, but they're not. They're more interested and genuinely appreciative of the fact that you're making the effort and giving it a go!

You want wealth? That's another very good destination. So sit right down, write yourself a plan and start creating your own kind of wealth. Ask yourself these three questions:

1.   What skills do you have to offer?
2.   What do you have to sell?
3.   Who can help?

Answer those questions and, whatever age you're at, whether young or old, you are starting on the road to reach your dreams. There are a million places to look. Try the newspapers, get on the internet, talk with your friends, and ravage the bookshelves for self-start information books and courses. You don't have to go out and buy Coca-Cola Schweppes! You just have to get started and just remember that every great business started its life as a small one.

Start small, think big, act sensibly. Remember the title of this book? It's: **Live BIG. Think LARGE. Act SENSIBLY**. These days, they even sell businesses in boxes. Yep, just like a fast food take-out, you've got everything you need to run your own business right there in a handy briefcase. Marketing materials, How To manuals, DVDs, hints, tips techniques, how to win business, how to do accounting, how to find customers - the whole lot is in the box for a few thousand pounds. An instant start on the journey to your dreams!

You want happiness? Now that's a fine destination. All you have to do is change the things in your life that are causing you distress and creating your current state of unhappiness. Tackle it because it won't ever go away, not until you act decisively and choose to do something about it. There I go again, evoking the immense power of choice. But that's how you change things and that's how you get things done. Not by talking about it, not even by thinking about it, but only by actually doing something about it. And it all comes down to you.

I know I'm going to be accused of making things sound all too simple, but to me, they are! I don't want to live a life that is riddled with complexity. I've seen what it does to people. I want to keep my life as simple as I possibly can so that I can move toward my goals, my dreams and my destinations with a clear mind and an even sharper focus. Let other people complicate things and drown themselves, metaphorically speaking, in tangles of their own confusion. Life is simple - it is only ever people that complicate things ... and they will - if you let them.

In my business life, the best successes I have ever had have been with the simplest things that I've ever created and the easiest to use programs that I have ever run. If you've ever tried to build flat packed furniture then you'll know exactly what I mean! Everybody likes things to be simple because that is pretty much how the world works. For something so awesomely complex the world is also an incredibly simple place. If you don't breathe, you'll die! How simple is that? If you don't eat, you'll starve. Sunshine is essential to life and so it goes on, with one thing following the next in a logical chain of events. The world's incredible complexity is masked by its basic simplicity. And you know, that's how business works too.

You start out with your dream (to make lots of money) that becomes your destination (early retirement with all the wealth you need to live life on your terms and do as you please). But the simplicity of that statement masks the complex requirements that may (and that is important!) be necessary to fulfil your dream. I say "may" quite deliberately because it could just be that you reach your destination and fulfil your dreams in just a few simple steps.

All you need is a really big idea ... a chocolate covered soft toffee candy bar called a Mars Bar created and even today still fuels a global business empire. A syrupy flavoured drink recipe turned Coca-Cola into a global giant. In just a few short years after an extensive relaunch Pringles turned the world of crisps on its head and they're not even made from potatoes!

You see, one simple idea and you are on your way to the destination of your dreams. Now, what's your destination and what dream have you got in mind?

> *"I can't change the direction of the wind, but I can adjust my sails to reach my destination."*
> Jimmy Dean, American entertainer & entrepreneur

Live BIG. Think LARGE. Act SENSIBLY.
How to make a fortune - without losing your friends!

Chapter 3

Sacrifice & compromise

"Nothing in the world is worth having or doing unless it means effort, pain, difficulty... I have never in my life envied a human being who led an easy life. I have envied a great many people who led difficult lives and led them well."
Theodore Roosevelt, 32nd President of the USA

I SAID earlier that you had to measure your success by what you had to give up to in order get it and I meant it. Success costs and you need to be sure that it is a price that you are willing to pay.

Many of my successful friends and global entrepreneurs have seen their relationships founder as they pursued success, or the goals of their destination. It is hard to buy into someone else's dream, even your closest friend's, your wife's, your husband's, or your partner's dreams. Unless you share the same dreams, hopes and ambitions things may well begin to unravel in your relationships. Brutal statement? No, it's purely a bald fact.

Being successful, or becoming successful, takes up and demands a lot of your time. In the beginning, it is always hard. You're green in the ways of business practice and inexperienced at running your own business. When you're starting out, the things you will one day do in a jiffy take two

---

or three times longer than necessary. Other things unexpectedly sideswipe you and steal your time, strangling your output and diminishing your BIG productivity. You can't know everything, and only a fool thinks they can do everything. Where's the 25-hour day when you most need it?

I'm not a terribly big believer in the "no pain, no gain" philosophy. I happen to believe that there is a lot you can gain from not flogging yourself to an exhausted standstill. You'll hear me say this often in the remainder of the book, but life is not about working harder ... it is about working smarter. It is about using your intelligence to minimise the effort that you have to make to succeed.

Take any process ... licking and sticking stamps on envelopes, for example. Fine, if you've only got 20 envelopes to handle. Not so fine if you're trying to mail 20,000 or 250,000 envelopes. So they invent a PPI (Printed Postal Impression) so that you can frank the envelopes quickly and get them out of the door in a fraction of the time it would take you to lick and stamp 25,0000 envelopes. And for the 20 envelopes? They invented peel and stick stamps to make it easier for you to do the job quicker. Peel and stick stamps make a lot more sense of your time. And in business, as it is in your life, time is everything. You cannot afford to waste a minute of what is easily the most precious resource you'll ever have ... your time.

One of the truly great things that I often hear from people who have chosen to work from home stands the idea of sacrifice on its head. Most people you talk to regret the fact that they never saw their children growing up. They were always too busy making money, brokering deals and tying up loose ends to ever bother about their children. The nanny did that, or the children's mother, or the partner took care of it, so what was there to worry about? The children were clothed and fed and their requirements were being taken care of.

Then, one day, you suddenly realise that your children have all grown up. They're young adults with hopes, dreams and ambitions, concerns, cares and worries and to you, they're almost total strangers. You haven't been part of their lives during those impressionable and early formative years and they know you almost as little as you know them. It comes as a big shock to many, many parents who have hit the success trail hard. You don't get to see, or experience all that your children need and by the time you wake up, it's too late and their childhood is over. I often wonder how many more times I will hear that deeply personal regret aired at meetings and seminars that I attend all over the world.

And yet for home entrepreneurs they tell me that not seeing their children grow up and spending time with them is a sacrifice they have never had to make! They see their children every day and often take them or collect them from school. They're "there", ready and waiting for chats and discussions and, as responsible parents they are able to contribute, help, shape and advise whenever guidance is needed. And the bond they form with their children is beyond value.

I can buy into that and have made strenuous efforts as a father to be there for my son. I didn't want my son to grow up with a "father he never knew". I want to be a part of his life and I want him to be a part of mine too. And I will do whatever I can to make that happen, as far as I am able to. Business can wait, but my son's birthdays, the theme park adventure and our holidays won't. When it comes to your children you really do need to think carefully about what you are prepared to give up in your quest to succeed. Most of us get few chances, ever, to be good parents. Chances are we'll get a lot more chances to be successful business people.

It took me a while to realise this simple truth, especially when I was working as a DJ in London, driving a taxi and parking cars to make ends meet. There wasn't a spare hour and sadly I didn't have a lot of time for my son back then. I do now and I make sure that I do now, so much so that I haven't missed a Sports Day, Nativity Play, School Trip or a promise that I've made to my son in the past six years. Not one.

Why am I telling you this? Look at it this way. You're driving your car and there's a blind bend up ahead. You're pootering along at 40mph, but you don't know what's around the bend. Your speed is steady and your awareness is keenly ready. Now, put yourself in the same scenario, driving your car toward the blind bend, but this time I tell you that there are two cyclists literally just around the corner on your side of the road. Aware of the danger, you adjust your speed accordingly so that you can safely negotiate the bend and the obstacle that you now know is there. If you know about it, you're aware of it and can plan and act accordingly and no one need get hurt. Finding out, on the other hand, can be a very expensive lesson with severe consequences. I know which position I'd rather be in.

There's a lot you may have to sacrifice to succeed in business, or to succeed in anything else come to that, but your children and personal relationships shouldn't have to be either of them. Work at it, be aware of it and it won't be.

If it teaches you nothing else, the pursuit of your dreams and success should teach you the art of compromise. You can't always hold out for what you want and you can't ever afford to be so unbending that you'd rather break in half than give in. If you do, you'll make a lot of enemies and in business you'll often find that enemies have very long memories!

Many years ago, I worked for a boss who was both a bully and a tyrant. He ruled the office by belittling colleagues and co-workers alike. He seemed to delight in making everyone feel small, usually over the smallest and most insignificant thing. One day, he took to task a very junior employee who had not long been with the company. He singled the poor guy out at a sales meeting and made fun of his hair, his glasses, his rather portly figure and lastly his inability to do the job for which he had been hired. It was an embarrassing display of tyranny and no one had the balls to stand up to this corporate bully. Utterly humbled and totally humiliated, the young man resigned his position shortly afterward.

Several years later, our company was invited to tender for a big slice of business. The company hadn't been doing too well and the win was necessary. We filed in to the boardroom with a presentation that was so good, so novel, so innovative and so wholly right that we felt we couldn't fail. We had pared costs to sensible parameters and we were ready to do what ever we had to do to win the business.

We sat at the boardroom table, eager to present our hot new ideas and brilliant new solution. After a short delay, the International Marketing Manager of the company made his entrance. My heart sank! Here before us was the very young man who had just a few years ago been crushed by the same man who was leading our team's presentation.

He smiled wryly at us and simply said, "Gentlemen, I have waited a long, long time for this moment."

Compromise doesn't mean giving in. It simply means that you may not get all that you've set your heart on, sometimes, that's no bad thing. It's rare that you're wholly right in anything. Few things it seems are "beyond a reasonable doubt" and everyone has a point of view. Compromise in business means arriving at the best possible solution when all points of view have been considered.

You'll know the number of times you've argued things one way, only to change your point of view half way through the argument or confrontation. That's when you smile, step down, hold your hands up and prove your worth. You're man enough, or woman enough, to make the right decisions, for all the right reasons and in business that can be a very big thing.

You bend a little and you gain a lot. People will remember your ability to compromise and they will respect you for it. Good people won't see it or try to exploit it as a weakness, which it most definitely isn't. Sensible business practice will steer you toward the right results far more often than pigheaded obstinacy ever will.

You must learn the art of compromise and know what you are willing to sacrifice if the sum of your actions is to ensure consistent success and earn the rewards you have imagined and set your heart upon achieving.

Chapter 4

What you must know

"Knowing others is wisdom; Knowing the self is enlightenment; Mastering others requires force; Mastering the self needs strength."
Lao Tzu, Founder of Taoism, 600-531 BC

SO YOU want to succeed, big style and there is a lot you are going to have to know, or, at the very least, come to terms with. Some of this valuable information you can read in books. Some you'll already have learned at the "school of life". Some you will have 'acquired' from the 'school of business' and the commercial experience and grounding that you've already had. Bits you'll pick up 'along the way'. You'll learn from others and expand your knowledge through courses, seminars, CDs, DVDs and contact with other professionals and business people.

But some of it you won't find in books or anywhere else for that matter because it has never been written down. That's the bit about you. In terms of your success and what you can and cannot achieve from this point forward, that is easily the most important part. You, and in the end, only you can determine and decide the level of success that is going to come your way.

Fail and it is all too easy to blame others. Chance,

circumstance, opportunity, other people, luck, the wrong day, the wrong horse, the wrong business, the wrong partner - if I had just a penny for every hard luck story of near misses that I have heard I'd be sitting on a shed full of gold bars! Take it from me you fail because you were prepared to accept failure. It was built into your plan. It's brutal, but it's true -success and/or failure is totally down to you. No one else and nothing else decides. You make it happen ... or you make sure it doesn't.

Enormous success on the other hand is a bit like the mystery of life itself. It depends a huge amount on all the right things coming together in exactly the right mix, at exactly the right time and in just the right proportions. It's a little bit of magic and a lot of hard work. It can demand long hours and selfless devotion to the exclusion of friends, family and social pleasures. I've got friends in business that have been married for nigh on thirty years. They've been running their own very successful businesses for most of that time and have holidayed together only twice in all of those years. That's what business can do to you ... if you let it.

Equally, I've got friends and acquaintances that have only recently discovered internet-driven businesses. They are running several highly successful operations, usually from home that are mostly automated and work like clockwork cash machines. They require very little in the way of maintenance, management and hands-on operation and deliver substantial sums of money - even when the business owner is on vacation, or away enjoying themselves doing other things.

The trick, as I've said, is not to work harder, but to find ways to work smarter. Think about it for a second. There is a finite amount of time that you have at your disposal. Let's say it's 7 chargeable hours a day. That makes up a 35 to 42 hour week, depending whether you choose to work 5 or 6 days. (Everybody needs a rest and recovery day!) Even if you optimise those hours and charge the most you can for them, say £200 an hour that's about £8000 a week. So far, so good. Tot them up and you could make £32,000 a month and that would give you just shy of £400,000 a year before tax, expenses and sundry overheads.

Now while that's good, it's not good enough. First of all, it's purely hypothetical. It works, but only in theory. Few of us can ever sell every working hour. Most of us would be lucky to sell half of the available hours in the example above, halving our gross earnings straightaway. Suddenly, £200,000 a year doesn't look quite so rosy before tax, expenses and overheads and before you factor in tiredness, possibly illness, economic downturns, client indecision and market whimsicality and whole bunch of other things that simply make the maths less and less attractive and the whole scenario less and less achievable.

How do I know this? Because I have tried to do it! What you're looking at in the above example is purely *linear income*. That means one income stream that is dependent on every single contributory factor being favourable, all of the time. As you know, life just isn't like that and things can, do and will get in your way.

What you need is *residual income* and multiple streams of it if you are to reach the kind of success you need to make all of your dreams come true without inheriting a fortune or winning the National Lottery! Residual income is money that is deposited into your bank account in large sums and earned without you having to do very much for it.

Don't worry - there's nothing dodgy about residual income and you will have earned the right to every penny that your businesses make. The difference is that instead of only selling your solitary hours once *(linear income)*, you have many businesses that sell many hours for you, many times over *(residual income)* - even when you're not working!

Does this sound too good to be true? How do you think I do it myself? I have many businesses that are working for me all of the time and I am constantly on the look out for new opportunities so that I can expand my own business portfolio with a range of new and relevant offerings. Many of my businesses are IT-oriented internet businesses that are run online. Why? Because the overheads are low, the shipping costs are negligible, the loyalty of customers is phenomenal and the need is always there. All a customer has to do is pay by credit card and press a button to download an instant software solution to their pressing problem. That puts money in my bank and a solution in their hands all at the simple press of a button.

Find enough customers at say £20 a download and you are on the road to making some serious money. 1,000 customers will generate £20,000-worth of turnover. 10,000 customers = £200,000-worth of turnover. 20 product lines all generating £20,000-worth of return and suddenly you're looking at £400,000. It's the same amount as I used in the example before but it isn't anywhere near as hard to do or achieve with the internet to help you. Just work at it, be streetwise and savvy, spot the need, answer the user's requirement and you've put yourself well on the road to riches and wealth. Doesn't that get you thinking? (It ought to get you champing at the bit, ready and eager to give it a go!)

The big thing you have got to realise is that you are unlikely to get rich simply by working for someone else, however kind and generous they happen to be. Of course, there are exceptions, but it is unlikely that those 'exceptions' are reading my book! City traders make huge salaries and often enjoy obscene bonuses ... but not all of them. Top Chairmen and industry executives often enjoy fabulous wealth and enormous pay packets ... but we can't all be so lucky! Financiers and people in the legal profession also enjoy huge earnings having worked their way up the ranks from junior to partner ... but they have worked hard to earn their positions and such opportunities are not available to all.

I'd like to add here that these few people who earn these mega salaries don't really get to enjoy them all that much. These people rarely have a lifestyle to match their fabulous earnings. Often, they suffer ill health, high blood pressure, stress and depression. Sure, they have nice cars, big flashy houses and money in the bank, but they leave for work at 4am Monday morning to drive up the M5 and M6 for a breakfast meeting in Manchester, then zig zag across the country to meetings all week, often staying in hotels, only to arrive home at 7pm on a Friday night absolutely cream-crackered! Great life, huh? At the weekend they want to rest... and all the kids want to do is go swimming or play football with their dad.

A good friend of mine, an international executive, is still tenderly recovering from a triple heart bypass. Sure he earns huge money. He travels the world, first class, but doesn't get to see much of it. You don't from an airport lounge or a hotel room. He lives with permanent stress and is away from his home for months at a time. He is only 47 and already his life is severely impaired.

Most of us are not given any such "golden opportunities". We have to make things work for ourselves and the best advice I can give you is that if you want to become seriously wealthy, or even just moderately more comfortable than you are so that money is neither an issue nor a problem, then you have to become your own boss.

John Paul Getty said it best when he said: *"You will never get rich working for someone else."* And the only way you will ever make any real money, apart from the few who feature in the examples I have given above, is to run your own business, or businesses.

Having made the decision to "go it alone" there are a few other things you need to know if you are to succeed in all the ways you desire.

1. All about yourself.

How ready are you? Are you prepared to put in the time and give up the hours to "buy" your dreams? It will cost and don't let anyone tell you anything different. It won't be easy and it will make big demands on you - your patience, endurance, stamina, strength and determination will all be pushed to the limit. The price could be high, but the question remains - is it a price that you are prepared to pay? Only you will ever know the answer, but if you are, the rewards could well be beyond anything you could seriously imagine.

It's often remarked by many of the most successful entrepreneurs that I meet that: *"The harder I try, the more successful I seem to be!"* For them, success drives success and successful people are like magnets ... they attract opportunities and every new success drives them into a different area, opening up even more opportunities that unsuccessful people never get to see or experience. Successful people all seem to experience this "cascade of success".

2. Where to find answers and information.

Successful entrepreneurs are by definition hugely resourceful people. They know where to look to find answers and they know how to make good and even great things happen regularly.

That means a relentless attention to detail and a thorough approach to success. Issues are opportunities, answers are bridges and information is essential to get you to the places you want to go. It happens because you make it and that only happens when you know where to look for answers and information.

3. Where to find a market.

You're not going anywhere until you find someone that wants to buy what you have to offer. And if you want to be immensely successful you have to do that in large numbers.

The internet is a powerful global market. It has made fortunes for people in record time and it continues to deliver. Google's founders are worth billions of dollars ... in just a matter of years. *MySpace* and *YouTube* both came from nowhere and in little more than a few months made their founders obscenely wealthy. *Friends Reunited* was a huge success built on a very simple idea. It took off, literally, after it was mentioned one afternoon on Steve Wright's Show on

Radio 2 causing the Friends Reunited server to crash as millions of people tried to access it!

What comes first, the idea or the market? The answer is that it's often a little bit of both, but many an idea has led to the downfall of many an individual and also broken the back of big companies because great ideas are of no use if no one wants to buy into them. As far as I'm concerned, Dead Certs don't exist. What happened to the Mini Disc for example? The "next big wave" in portable and recordable music punted so heavily by Sony is now a history lesson. Dasani, Coca-Cola's answer to the water question was a PR disaster from which the company is still working hard to recover.

All you can ever do is test, test and test again to make sure that what you have to offer is what people need. Pick yourself a winner and the cash register will never stop spinning.

Chapter 5

The true value of money

*"The real measure of your wealth is how much you'd be worth
if you lost all your money."*

Anonymous

"MONEY ISN'T everything!" Just try telling that to someone that hasn't got any. I can assure you that it cuts a pretty hollow note. But then again, few would argue that money is everything. Quite simply, it's not.

What money does is provide the bridge to all things. With it, you can have practically everything you want. Without it, in the civilised world, you can do nothing, own nothing and go practically nowhere. Still think money doesn't matter?

Sure, the best things in life are free. Says who and do you really believe that? If you do, then business and commerce is not for you because everything it can do for you and all that it can give you are not for you, unless of course you are such a generous soul that you'll simply give it all away.

People who are fabulously wealthy can afford to be generous. They're not worried where the next ten pence is coming from! And yet I see and hear of amazing acts of charity by people who have so little to give. In very real terms, just like the fabulously wealthy, these people understand the real value of money.

Money is important and you should never pretend otherwise. But it should never become your all-consuming focus, the one thing that dominates your life, the obsession that fills every waking hour. Make money your god and you'll be cheapening the meaning of your life. Your life should be bigger than simply the accumulation of massive wealth because the whole point of money is not how much you have, but what you can actually do with it.

The fact is that money will have a greater influence on your life than almost anything you can think of. Until you've acquired enough, it will be your driver, your motivator and even your passion. Then, as things fall into place and you acquire your dreams and live the life you've longed for, money comes to mean less and less to you. And that's pretty much true of everyone I've ever met that has truly understood the value of money.

However, I've met some very questionable individuals along the way that have acquired reasonable even outrageous wealth but who never really truly understood what money was about. They pretended to, but you could always see through the veneer of their pretence. Whatever they gave, they gave grudgingly and with reluctance and anything they gave came at a price - the old *quid pro quo* routine ... I will only do something for you, if you do something in return. They were and are some of the loneliest people I have ever met.

What use is money if you don't use it? Use it to do some good. Use it to make other people happy. Use it to make yourself happy. Use it to give others a start in life. Build something of value with it because that is its only real purpose - to create tangible effects that give life and meaning to chains of events and circumstances.

How many times do you read in the newspapers about people that have lived sparingly and then died "penniless and alone", only to discover when the truth finally emerges that they were sitting on millions? Recently, I read a story of man who had died without making a will. He had no dependants, no relatives and no children. No visitors ever came to his dilapidated house in all the time that the neighbours could remember. When his house was searched after the owner's death they found millions of pounds in cash in boxes all over the house yet the man had lived like a penniless pauper.

Call me cruel, even insensitive, but what a waste! It was a waste of a life and a total waste of the money too. The man never understood the value of money and nobody had ever showed him how to use one of the most powerful tools you can ever get your hands on.

Fear can do that to you. It's easy to become afraid that you will lose the lot and then what will you have to live on? So you protect what you've got by trying not to spend it. You trade the life you could have led, for fear of losing what you've got and all that you could have been and should have enjoyed is overshadowed by the fear of failure. The life you end up living is not the one you wanted, nor the one you could have had.

Someone perhaps a little wiser than me wrote in his book *Born Rich* that you must *"love people, but learn to use money"*. That man was Bob Proctor and it is a sentiment that I have bought into. People are the coldest, cruellest and often the most unreliable currency on the planet, but they are by far the most important currency you will ever get to handle.

By currency, what do I mean? Everybody you ever meet has a rate of exchange, a value, just like a currency. At its most basic, there are things you will do for money and things you would never dream of. That gives you a value. It also gives you ethics, integrity and honesty and I will deal with those issues later. In the cold light of day, there will be people (hopefully, lots of them!) who will deserve your investment in them and equally there will be people that simply do not. I'm not setting myself up as any sort of god, judge or jury when I write that statement. I am simply a businessman who is calling life as I find it. Not everyone deserves your help and assistance, your kindness and concern and only a naïve person would ever believe otherwise.

Just as you are looking for solutions that will make you wealthy, you are also looking, either consciously or unconsciously, for people that you can relate to and work with. People you can buy into who share your values, hopes, dreams, fears and philosophy. People who can help you to drive your dreams forward and also people that you can help to realise their own dreams and ambitions. But here's the thing with the 'currency of people' - there's no "rate of return". You're not even looking for any ROI (Return On your Investment). You're just happy to "make the investment" and see what happens. And at that precise moment, you truly understand the real value of money and what it means to use it well and wisely.

In my life, I have had a lot of jobs. I've been a DJ, a taxi driver, a car park attendant, a labourer and a good few things in between. Not all of them were well paid, but practically all of them were enjoyable. In some of my really dark times, I drove a taxi and often picked up senior executives, company chairmen and industry super achievers. Most could be rude and dismissive. After all, to them I was a "nobody" without a story worth hearing. One day, a well-dressed and clearly powerful executive jumped into my cab in Haymarket in London's, West End and I drove him back to his £2m home in Buckinghamshire.

We struck up a conversation and he asked me if I enjoyed my job. I told him that I did and he replied that he had once been a taxi driver himself back in his own country. It turned out that here was a man who had seen it all, had it all and lost the lot! After his downfall, he had been a window cleaner, a milkman and a taxi driver, but he had never lost his zest for life and his sense of what was important. Nor had he lost his wife and children, a fact he considered to be the most important thing he had held onto.

From his own dark times he had risen once again to become the CEO of a major photoelectricals giant here in the UK. And the lesson his losses had taught him was to learn to listen because even the most ordinary man still has a story to tell and that story is worth hearing. In his own words, his fall had taught him to be humble, respect other people's situations and given him a clearer understanding of how to respond, react and interact with other people.

It had made it easier for him to understand how to help others and shown him why he needed to. As a boss in a huge multinational organisation he felt his experiences at the bottom had made him a better manager and, perhaps more significantly, a much better person. Throughout his trials at the bottom of the pile, he had come to understand the true value of money and its relationship in people's lives.

I am reminded, often, of the value of money whenever I see my former wife's father. When I was desperate, distressed and confused about my direction and trying hard to hold onto my sanity and my marriage, he was an IT contractor in the boom period. He was making a handsome £700 a day and never missed a chance to get after me for my own failures, weaknesses and lack of success.

There I was a humble taxi driver and, at the time, there he was, a hotshot businessman with a sure and steady contract. But as you know, there is no job for life and nothing lasts forever. Soon the good times were over and my father in law's contract came to an end. He was out of work for almost two years and eventually secured himself a job ... as a taxi driver. His success had evaporated and with bad grace he joined the ranks of the wage-earning mortals. The very people he had despised and had looked down upon were now his workmates and colleagues. He has never recovered the loftiness of his former position, nor has he come to understand the currency of people, but I suspect that he now understands the real value of money.

I use the story to illustrate the point that life is a people business and people matter more than money ever will. Money's good, in fact it's great, but only if it is used to make good things happen.

Make it work for you and make sure it works for others too and I am certain your life will be full to overflowing. Good things grow when the right seeds are planted creating consistent streams of opportunity and a steady stream of success.

Chapter 6

What is HIE?

"Honesty is the first chapter in the book of wisdom."
Thomas Jefferson, 3rd US President,
Author of the Declaration of Independence, 1762-1826

THERE'S A lot of things you are going to need to make your mark, in fact any sort of mark, in business. But there are some things you simply cannot manage without.

I personally am a great believer in HIE!

What, you may ask, is HIE? It is simply an acronym for *Honesty, Integrity and Ethics* (HIE) and that's something that I've used repeatedly as a barometer to guide my own success and as an internal chant, a mantra, to keep my feet firmly planted on the floor. You see, probably like you, I have worked with, met, encountered and locked horns with some of the most unpleasant people that life ever put on the planet. They've done things and been responsible for things that defy logic, description and sometimes even explanation. In the same breath, I've worked with, been partnered by, joint ventured with and been associated with some of the very finest individuals that ever drew breath in this life or any other. They are my kind of people.

Honesty. Does it really matter? I guess not to somebody who is essentially dishonest, but for my own part and that of a good many people in business, I think it does matter. It matters a great deal.

Recently, I was asked to consider a joint venture opportunity with a supplier who was promoting a product that clearly would not work here in the UK. No matter what you did, you would not be able to make this product work in the way it was intended. I knew this and so did the supplier.

He was working on the shaky assumption that people who bought the product wouldn't complain so his returns level would be low and he would still be able to make money. The truth is that few people ever do complain and ask for a refund. Most people just 'can't be bothered', but they will never buy a bad product again and a dodgy seller only ever gets one chance to make a fool out of anyone.

That's not, has never been and will never be how I work. My customers matter to me, all of them. They are my business and they are my future and if they're not happy, then I'm not happy either.

So, I turned the supplier down flat much to his dismay and sheer disbelief. He couldn't understand why I wouldn't want to be associated with his venture since the objective of his business was *"to make money any way that I can buddy!"* I wish him well.

I can't look at life that way and I certainly couldn't, can't and won't run my businesses in any way that is remotely dishonest. I don't want to make money in any way that I can. Where is the joy in such a statement? And just who is the victim with such a warped philosophy? It's your friends and your family, your partner, your wife or husband and all the people that mean the most to you. And it's your customers, the very people you should be looking out for and protecting.

In my businesses I work with a lot of people. I share opportunities with them and structure a variety of trading relationships that provide mutual benefits to all parties. Much depends on trust especially when you have agreed to a 5% share of gross sales, or a 40% share of a joint venture product. Trust is a very big thing in my business and I can honestly say that I have never and would never short-change anybody in any deal that I have ever negotiated. It wouldn't even cross my mind. In the same way, I hope that everybody that I have ever brokered a deal with has been entirely honest with me and coughed up exactly the right share. I don't know for sure, but that's what I want to believe.

To my mind, honesty makes the wheels of business spin smoothly. It makes me feel proud of who I am, what I have achieved and all that I can do and I wouldn't want it any other way. My word is my bond and you should do everything you can to make sure that yours is too. People will respect you for it and your customers will love you for it. Satisfied customers keep on coming back because they trust you and delighted partners are never shy about telling others that you're a decent guy to do business with. That's how success breeds success and great fortunes are made because everything is built on all the right principles. And there is no better way that I know of to market yourself successfully than by word of mouth.

Your good name and your excellent reputation for dealing honestly will sweep all before it, winning you contracts and customers for many years to come. Honesty is a business jewel. I urge you to guard it wisely and use it well.

Integrity. The dictionary describes integrity as *"the quality of being honest and having strong moral principles."* We've dealt with the honesty part, so let's look at the integrity bit.

You'll get nowhere meaningful in this life if your attitude is to "better and best" everyone else. All you'll ever get is eternal and consistent disappointment. The more times you try to make everyone else a loser the more you'll make yourself a loser and that is not a nice way to live your life.

Do not *"compare yourself with others ... for always there will be greater and lesser persons than yourself."* Desiderata, a poem, a prayer, an inspired piece of wisdom and a sharply truthful commentary on life written, it is believed, by Max Ehrmann and published in 1927, put it better than I ever could. The moment that you believe yourself to be supremely important is the moment you're heading for an enormous fall. Conceit and arrogance have little place in the armoury of a successful businessperson. Life isn't about wringing every penny out of everyone you meet and battering the biggest discount out of every supplier. Life is bigger than that and if you can see the bigger picture I think you'll enjoy a lot more success. You'll certainly get a lot more satisfaction out of the things you do and the business ventures that you engage in.

Integrity to me means being the person you want to become. It means dealing openly, honestly and fairly with everyone you meet and each situation that you encounter. Sometimes, it means backing people, even suppliers, when they've let you down and failed to live up to your expectations. That's life and occasionally it will let you down, but you shouldn't ever let it put you down. Real people and really successful people are always bigger than that.

Whenever you compare yourself to others you're invariably going to be disappointed. You may not have the house, car, helicopter, bank balance, stud farm or even sun tan that your closest competitor or archrival has, but hey, take at look at the positives and concentrate on what you have got! Too many people spend far too much time looking over their shoulders and watching for the shadow that is creeping up behind them. They're never satisfied and far too much energy is wasted on fruitless comparisons. Insane jealousy creeps in and integrity flies out of the window in a mindless quest to better someone else, in fact anyone else!

Do you really think the person you're comparing yourself to cares? I doubt it and does it matter anyway? If it stunts your growth and deflects your concentration from the task of running your businesses successfully then you are simply wasting your energy, wasting your time and belittling everything you can possibly achieve and accomplish. It's demeaning and I urge you never to do it. If all you ever do is compare yourself to others then you are dwarfing your own success and you will never become a big player, or that larger than life person you want to be.

Just keep a sense of proportion about all things, deal openly, honestly and fairly with everyone and build your reputation as a businessperson with integrity in all that you touch, handle and do. Do that and I think your success will fly right off the scale.

Ethics. These are the moral principles that govern a person's, a group's, or a business's behaviour. I have strong principles, as I've already explained and there are market sectors that I simply wouldn't touch even though I'm sure there is good money to be made from them.

But once again, you have to know the facts and work with

the correct business intelligence before you can make an informed decision about what you will or will not do. Not so long ago there was (and still is) a huge outcry about Nike's "exploitation" of the Far East and their decision to use "slave labour" for pennies, nickels and cents to create products that Nike then sold for many tens of pounds, euros, dollars and yen. Wilful and nasty press reporting that simply did not provide a balanced view of the facts fanned public outrage. The press simply did not tell the whole story and the public lashed out at Nike, boycotting their products and staging public demonstrations against this "human injustice".

I lunched recently with a senior Nike brand manager who had spent much of his life working for the company in the Far Eastern "sweat shops". He had a very different view of the ethics and motives behind Nike's and many other giant western companies who had moved their manufacturing processes to the Far East. His was the balanced view that the press had signally failed to give and highlighted these companies huge investment in developing the economic infrastructure of these "fringe" countries. He illustrated how they had changed the social map, elevated standards overall and created much good, at a cost that was equable to the standard wage that was being earned in that country they had chosen.

I don't want to get into heated debate over the rights and wrongs of Western capitalism marching into Third World countries. I just want to make the point that there are many sides to every story and wherever ethics are concerned the moral high ground may not always provide either the truth or the answer!

I like to think that I am an ethical businessman and that all of what I do, or pretty much most of it, does a lot of good for a lot of people. And along the way, I make a great deal money from what I do, without hurting, harming, restricting, or belittling anyone. I don't have a problem with profit. That is what you are in business to do - make a profit. Profit is healthy, but I do have something of a problem with obscene profits and outrageous profiteering that is derived with more than a whiff of dishonesty.

Arbitrage, the buying and selling of securities, currencies and commodities in different markets to take advantage of different prices for the same thing is a whole different ball game. George Soros, the financial speculator, made himself famous for breaking the Bank of England. He sold short more than $10 billion worth of UK pounds, profiting from the Bank of England's and the Government's idiotic belief that they could fix the rate of sterling against foreign currencies. Eventually, the Bank of England was forced to withdraw from the European Exchange Rate Mechanism (ERM) and significantly devalue the pound, earning George Soros an estimated US$ 1.1 billion. Nothing wrong with it and all power to him - I take my hat off to him. He has of course since used his enormous wealth to encourage fringe nations to become 'open societies,' promoting freedom of commerce and tolerance of new ideas, new thinking and more liberal behaviour.

Some would argue that the price is what the market is prepared to pay. If you can live with it, that's fine and you'll surely make a lot of money. I can't and choose not to, but yet I still manage to make a lot of money! I sell honestly, I price properly and I profit fairly and my *HIE* would never allow me to do business any other way!

But of course you must always decide what works best for you. Somehow, fleecing your friends, colleagues, family and customers has never seemed that attractive to me. There has to be a better way and I think I've found it. I hope that you will too.

So, just how do you set about making a large amount of money?

Well, you can start by searching junk shops, antique houses and hidden galleries in out of the way places because, apparently, there are over 100 Turner masterpieces somewhere that have never been accounted for. Find one and you'll probably pocket a few million!

Perhaps you could broker a deal the like of which I heard about just recently. A well-known UK company with lots of money to spend on its advertising and public reach marketing committed to a nationwide campaign. The actual cost of the campaign, so I'm told, was £2.5million. The bill when it reached the client was a gigantic £12.5 million. Someone, somewhere along the way had made a sizeable chunk of change! Ethical, reasonable, decent and honest? I'm, sorry, but I must leave you to make your own mind up on that one!

Or, more likely, you develop a product, service, solution or application that everybody wants. You market it wisely and sell it well at a reasonably healthy profit. You reach a global audience of say 10 million and make a net profit from every sale of just a miserly £5. Do that and you've just put £50 million into your bank account.

Of those three choices, I know which option I would choose and I also know that I make it sound so easy, but – and you have to trust me on this - it really is and can be that easy!

While I may not be an absolute example of virtue (who among us is?) and yes I've done some things that I'm not proud of, business has made me grow up and take stock of who I am, what I've got and who I want to become. And I know that it can work that way for you too, if you let it.

"Integrity is doing the right thing, even if nobody is watching."
Anonymous

"Never let your sense of morals get in the way of doing what's right."
Isaac Asimov, Writer & Biochemist, 1920-1992

Live **BIG.** Think **LARGE.** Act **SENSIBLY.**
How to make a fortune - without losing your friends!

Chapter 7

What you need to accept

"Why do you stay in prison when the door is so wide open?
Jalal ad-Din Rumi, Persian poet, 1207-1273

THE FIRST thing you need to wrap your head around is that being in business and becoming a success is not just a walk in the park! As I said somewhere earlier - if it was easy, everybody would be doing it ... and they're not! Ever wondered why?

That's a simple question to answer. Practically everybody wants everything to be easy and it's not. It just isn't. A S Neill, a British educationist, started an experimental kind of school called Summerhill, which became famous for its liberal approach to education for its students. For example, students attended lessons because they wanted to, not because they had to. No one checked and no one forced the students to do anything they didn't want to. By and large, the students accepted the "rules" of the school by their own choice. They either agreed and co-operated, or they didn't. They worked out, for themselves, the merits of appropriate behaviour and the consequences of unacceptable behaviour. The students set the standards and created the school's working pattern of behaviour and study. Summerhill worked because the students wanted it to and they set about making the school a successful educational environment.

Live **BIG.** Think **LARGE.** Act **SENSIBLY.**
How to make a fortune - without losing your friends!

The students evolved their own value system and by proxy the teachers had to be up to the task because if they didn't teach well no one would turn up for their lessons! It's an interesting idea which sets the teacher up as a "floating currency" whose skills find their own value and create a rate of exchange in the "interest" they are able to foster in the students they teach. Perhaps there is much that today's educational establishments could learn from such a practice?

However, A S Neill coined a phrase that has stuck with me ever since I first read it many years ago. He simply said: *"There are no bad children. Only ever bad parents."* I use that statement to amplify what I have already said - *everybody wants everything to be easy and it's not. It just isn't.* Parenting is a classic case in point. Badly behaved children, unruly little tyrants, rude and aggressive children are the way they are because their parents give up too easily on parenting properly. They want it to be "easy". Let's face it, it is hard to keep on keeping on reinforcing what is good, appropriate and acceptable behaviour in a child who simply doesn't know any better. Easier to ignore it, or even patronise it: *"Ooh, our Tommy can be a proper little rascal, Can't he?"* Well he always will be until you take responsibility as a parent and do something about it! See what I mean when A S Neill said it? *No bad children - only ever bad parents.*

Yes, it is hard to keep on "correcting" behaviour. Hard to instil values, morality, dignity, ethics and all of those good things that sit at the heart of any responsibly behaved adult ready to take a worthy place in society. But it is so worth the effort! Because the rewards are phenomenal. No child ever asks to be born. That was your choice and it is also your duty to help the child(ren) you brought in to this world to become the most complete adults they are capable of becoming. If that didn't strike home already, I'm going to say it again, just so you'll hear: *"It is your duty as a parent to help the child(ren) you brought in to this world to become the most complete adults they are capable of becoming."*

As you've guessed, I am big on responsibility, standing up to be counted and shouldering the burden! If you are to succeed in business, then I think that you will need to be too.

To open this chapter I said that being in business and becoming a success is not the easiest thing you'll ever do. It simply isn't and you can be in business all of your life and still not become a success! What? Not possible! Oh yes, very possible and, unless you're ready to listen up and listen hard, very likely to happen.

This is what you need to know, accept, internalise and manage successfully if you are to succeed in the biggest style imaginable:

1.   It isn't easy to run a successful business.
2.   You need to think smart, all of the time.
3.   You need to listen and not just with your ears!
4.   Keep every channel of communication fully open.
5.   Avoid negativity and the "harbingers of gloom".
6.   If you don't know it, find someone that does!
7.   Learn from every setback.
8.   Improve yourself in every possible situation.
9.   Build your business with dignity and style if you want it to last.
10. Work only ever as hard as you actually need to...

I have seen so many companies go to the wall because

they did not act sensibly and I refer you once again to the title of this book. Just to refresh your memory it's this: **Live BIG. Think LARGE. Act SENSIBLY.**

Entrepreneurs often start out strong with a great idea, or two. Orders flood in and so does the money and everything is rosy for a while. Yes, the chant and the excuses are: *"There's always plenty more where that came from, boys! So, let's enjoy ourselves. We're young and you only get to live once!"* Yes, you may only get to live once, but while you're alive you can get to pay many times over, I'm afraid.

So these young bucks, flush with success, buy expensive flashy cars that lose 40% and more of their value as soon as they are driven off the forecourt and have the resale value of a broken house brick! Trust me, a Porsche, Lamborghini or Ferrari looks great … on the pages of a magazine, unless you can truly afford to behave and spend like money doesn't matter! Any such car is practically worthless to a sinking business.

Personally, I drive an Aston Martin. Why? Because I love the brand of car and it gives me everything I ever wanted from the idea of luxury car ownership. I can afford to own such a car. The success of my businesses sees to that and as long as I can afford to pay for it, comfortably, I will go on owning and driving an Aston Martin. It is the one statement of luxury that I actually allow myself.

Extravagant (and often unnecessary) business premises luxuriously appointed with finely crafted furniture and all the trimmings of success makes about as much sense as heating a house and leaving all of the windows open! Unless you actually need the space, why are you paying for it? Every square metre costs you money, whether anybody ever uses it, or not. Flashy premises can be a huge drain on a company's balance sheet and I know of a lot of top earners who are worth many millions and they actually work from the comforts of their own home!

Then there's the "expenses" to account for, balance in the books and ultimately pay for. Too many companies large and small, both fledgling and mature, have no real idea about the cost of their expenses - taxis, paper, phone calls, computers, software and so on. They never check, so they never know. Expenses is a hot topic with many a marketing guru that I've ever listened to. Check your expenses on a monthly or even more frequent basis and you'll close a hole that could easily be bleeding your business dry and quietly costing you a fortune.

Then there's the big issue of taxation. Inevitably, it comes around and you have to make provision for it. Inept business people fail to do this and without beating around the bush, they deserve to fail. It's an irresponsible way to run your life and it is a juvenile way to run any business not to make accountable preparation for every debt that is likely to occur.

What's left when you've prepared for what you know is coming is yours to take out … and, in the beginning, in the early days of a business, it probably won't amount to much. It's not that long ago that I was awakened early one evening by a supplier standing on my porch asking me to buy his gold Rolex Oyster with its diamond studded face from him so that he could pay his tax bill. It had cost him £23,000 a few months earlier. To me it was worth no more than a child's Lego building brick. Such unnecessary flashiness at that moment of desperation had no value and I couldn't help him.

I am however happy to report that he did 'get out jail'. I never found how, but he is still trading successfully today and continuing to proudly wear the "badges of his success" - flashy cars, smart cut suits and the expensively permanent suntan.

But the biggest thing that brings a business down is the public's changing tastes and preferences. Suddenly, a market dies and its customers have moved onto something else. What became I wonder of all the copier giants that once flooded big businesses with stacks of photocopiers that I seem to remember always got broken around Christmas with too many secretaries, PAs and office staff all too eager to jump on them to display their "private wares" for posterity to see? The market went and many of the companies probably went with it. There are very few markets and particularly over the past decade that are built to last forever.

When the wind turns, there are often huge casualties. Remember DEC, Digital Equipment Corporation? Had a chance in their hands to outstrip and pre-empt Google. It was right there, in their hands and their management blew it, leaving Compaq to pick the debris and discarded husk of a once great global giant.

What of the fax machine? It has virtually gone with barely a whimper taking many companies into oblivion with it. The Psion organiser and the Time Manager, the 14.4 and 28.8 Kbps modems, dot matrix printers - the list is endless and growing all of the time. But to survive in turbulent and changing times, companies have to be nimble, agile, flexible, versatile and informed. Is that you? If it's not, then your business life could be very short lived.

A successful printing firm once used to do an awful lot of work for me. Their work was good and they were very successful. They operated on fair margins and were good at winning new business by providing excellent customer service. Unfortunately, their business sense didn't stretch to reading the future too well and they invested heavily in bigger premises, new plant and an expensive, flashy new four-colour film reproduction and separation system. Their investment cost a small fortune and they borrowed heavily to finance the debt. Within a few months Photoshop had changed the world. Film separation was history and their expensive kit was redundant. Loss followed loss as they tried to compete on price to keep the factory full and the new presses rolling. Deadlines slipped, customers got angry and left, and within a year the business went bust. Ambition had ripped the heart out of their own success and sent them spinning into oblivion. It was all very sad.

Why do companies fail? Usually it's for these or a combination of these reasons:

Poor targeting - poor companies fail to find the hungriest crowd.

Lousy pricing - public perception is the key to successful pricing. Pitch it too low and you could struggle to meet demand. Set it too high and you won't sell enough to cover costs and overheads.

Failure to plan properly - you've got to know where you're going and how to make it happen.

Inept management - even great companies can be brought down by clowns in positions of power and influence. Ask DEC!

Expenses - check them regularly and often if you want to keep your sanity and your suit!

Lack of reinvestment - take too much out of the business and it will buckle because it won't have sufficient funds and reserves to meet its commitments. You should always be looking to reinvest a certain amount of revenue in your business to reskill your people, update your systems, sharpen your cutting edge and send out a clear competitive message. If you don't do this, your business will start to die from the inside because no one is breathing life and purpose back into it.

But essentially there are four very big "DON'TS" that every successful businessperson needs to be aware of and accept:

a.   Don't ever get complacent!

It is true that the higher you climb, the further you have to fall and falls can be spectacular with effects that last longer than your success. Take a long look at Gerald Ratner. One throwaway comment, stupidly said at a business function, cost him his life's work and led to the entire collapse of his business empire.

Although glitzy and a little tacky, Ratner's shops were very popular with the public ... until Gerald Ratner made a truly ill fated speech at the Institute of Directors in April 1991. What he actually said was:

> *"We also do cut-glass sherry decanters complete with six glasses on a silver plated tray, all for £4.95. People say "How can you sell this for such a low price?" I say, because it's total crap."*

He went on to say that some of the earrings his shops sold were *"cheaper than an M&S prawn sandwich but probably wouldn't last as long."*

Reported widely by the media, that speech wiped an estimated £500m from the value of the company. The public rightly felt insulted and let down and the end of the business was inevitable.

b.   No business or businessperson is ever "bullet proof"!

Can't happen to you? Don't you believe it! If I had a pound for everyone that had said that at some time in their lives, once again, I'd be sitting on a royal fortune. It very much can happen to you - often when you least expect it and from areas that you would never have predicted. That's life. What do you do when the business partner you have trusted for so long, for years and years, one day empties the joint business account and clears off with all of the business cash, its savings and its reserves? All the tax, all the VAT, all the salaries and all the profits, cleared in an instant by someone that you had trusted completely.

Can't happen to you? Believe that and, trust me, it will. Who would have thought or could have predicted that Vodafone would have turned its back on The Carphone Warehouse to bed a better deal with Phones 4U? CPW shares have slumped in value, other mobile operators are "reviewing" their CPW deals and a once seriously healthy business faces an uncertain future ... and no one saw it coming. No business is ever bullet proof.

c.   Don't ever put it all back in.

You can't take it all out, but you should never put it all back in again either. Things do go wrong and life is, at best, unpredictable.

A businessman I know worked hard for 18 years to build up his name and reputation and consistently delivered excellence to all of his customers. He took very little from the business and was proud to assert quietly, when pressed, that he was "cash rich". His business went from strength to strength and he expanded, carefully at first. Then he got a little more ambitious and, geographically, it became hard for him to be "everywhere all at once". The strain got to him and he fell ill. His trusted lieutenants let him down badly and from a position of strength his business crumbled and all of his cash reserves were swept away when he finally went bankrupt.

He'd had the money for years to have paid off his modest mortgage. He didn't even do that and when the day of reckoning came, he lost his house with the swimming pool that had been his pride and joy. He downsized his house and his entire lifestyle to pay off his creditors and now, with his illness, there is no way back for him. He's 54 years old and finished. It wasn't that he put it all back in. He just didn't take out what was rightfully his and paid a heavy price for his own mis-management.

The lesson is simple. Use the money you make wisely and make it work for you properly in every way that you need to. There is always today, but who knows whether you will have a tomorrow?

Money is made to be used and when you put it back into circulation you stand a much better chance of making good and possibly even great things happen.

d.   Don't ever believe that you can do everything.

You can't. No one can and you will kill yourself trying! You're not superman. None of us are. You must learn to use your time wisely, not by working harder but by always working smarter. You have a finite number of hours in a day, a week, a month and a year. Your task is to use them as wisely and as profitably as possible by optimising the value of every hour. The more people you can get to do things reliably for you, the more revenue streams you have feeding into your business, so that, effectively, you can sell each hour many times over. The maths is simple:

You are 1 person = 1 hour = 1 profit stream because you can only do 1 thing at a time.

But if you engage the services of say 60 people in that same 1 hour = 60 profit streams.

You can't do everything and seriously successful business people don't even try. What they do is try to find reliable generals, lieutenants, corporals, field staff and foot soldiers who can help them to achieve more simply by getting more done.

You also need to realise and accept that things will change for you and around you. Being in business often exerts a big toll on human relationships. The more successful you become the bigger the strain you are likely to be put under. You move away from your roots. You change your opinions and your thinking. And that's when relationships can start to founder, however strong they may appear or have been. If you're aware of it, then you're ready for it, but only you can decide if you want pay the price of being successful in business, or even being in business, by seeing your personal relationships crumble and your old friends disappear. It can only happen, if you allow it to happen.

"The minute you settle for less than you deserve, you get even less than you settled for."

Maureen Dowd, Columnist, The New York Times

Live **BIG.** Think **LARGE.** Act **SENSIBLY.**
How to make a fortune - without losing your friends!

Chapter 8

Why everyone hates a winner!

"Hatred is the coward's revenge for being intimidated."
George Bernard Shaw, Irish playwright & Nobel Prize winner,
1856-1950

IT'S SOMETHING that I have always found hard to explain and very difficult to understand. Oddly enough, it would seem to me that it is a peculiarly English or British characteristic. Nowhere else that I've travelled and I've pretty much covered most of the globe seems to hate success as much as we British. And we hate it with a passion that is ugly to the point of criminality!

It seems to me that there are many things you can do and get away with and in judgement you will be pardoned and forgiven for some pretty wicked crimes. But the one thing people will never forgive you for is your success.

In the years (and it's not really that long ago) before mobile phones became a "cannot do without" item and such a passionate part of everyone's life, I had the good misfortune to be the owner and user of a brick-like piece of mobile machinery. You had to charge it for practically 4 days to get 80 minutes of battery life out of it. Put it in your pocket and you walked like Quasimodo because it really did weigh the proverbial ton! Drop it on your foot and you would break it -

Live BIG. Think LARGE. Act SENSIBLY.
How to make a fortune - without losing your friends!

not the phone, your foot! It was almost the size of a telephone kiosk piece of machinery but it was portable (just!) and it did the job (much better than you would have expected!).

However, I had to use the phone on my travels to keep in touch with suppliers, progress enquiries, deal with issues and run my business while on the move. Practically everywhere I went in England, I was jostled in the street and in the railway station by people who deliberately walked into me, simply because I was using a mobile phone. I had something they didn't have and probably couldn't afford and that singled me out as a target. What sort of a mentality does that? What sort of unstable people behave like that?

Maybe you're going to write and tell me that you experienced the same sort of infantile behaviour in your own country. Perhaps the French, Germans, Italian, Spanish and Americans can be just as spiteful and small-minded. I don't know, because I never came across it. Only here, in England, was I ever made to feel like a "successful social leper" all because I had the front to use a mobile phone, a thing that I often wish now had never been invented! How did we ever manage without mobile phones? The answer is - we didn't!

But now, everywhere you go, in trains, restaurants, planes, boats, lounges, in the street, in bars, cafes, shops - there is no hiding place, all you can ever hear is the constant babble of inane drivel. Sure, they all talk ... about nothing! They say that 86% of email is spam. I personally think that the percentage of "inanely irrelevant" mobile phone conversations is probably even higher than that!

Why is it that in the "golden days" before mobile phones

we would only ever call home if we were going to be over half an hour late, just to make sure no one would worry. Now we call and say: *"I'll be home in 5 minutes!"* The mobile phone truly has changed our lives, but often it has not been for the better!

These days, it is fast becoming a bad idea to be successful and to wear the badges of your success. Cars and houses of successful entrepreneurs are vandalised. Expensive watches and jewellery are torn from their owners in broad daylight. And just about everyone hates a winner.

But why is that? Where are we going wrong and can it ever be put right? These are enormous questions that deserve the insight of minds far greater than mine to unravel, but I have never been one to leave things hanging and I do have my own ideas I'd like to offer you.

Jealousy clearly has a lot to do with it. People can be unbelievably spiteful and viciously small-minded whenever they see someone who is clearly more successful and enjoying something that they simply cannot have or never will get to own or enjoy. Logic seems to fly out of the window and a grasping kind of desperation to wound and hurt takes over. They have to find fault and either the person "doesn't deserve it", or must have made it through criminal activity, or, more likely, it was "pure luck". Maybe they just inherited their wealth - they certainly didn't earn it!

Where it comes from, I am at a loss to know. Are all of these people just poor losers who simply want to beat up the victor, rather than applaud and champion the winner's skill? That said how can anyone hate Roger Federer or the great Pete Sampras. But they do and they did. They hate Federer's invincibility and his perfection. Somehow they despise the fact that he is richly gifted, unbelievably modest and a very worthy champion who will in time become the world's greatest-ever tennis player. They hated Sampras because he was a ruthlessly efficient champion who shared nothing of his soul for the public to feast their insatiable desire for scandal on. Isn't that a truly sad state of affairs? That the sole aim of the media machine is to belittle greatness and reduce it to its most common levels?

What makes a spiteful driver slam their car door hard into the Ferrari that (unfortunately) has dared to park next to them? (Remember, the Ferrari was there first!) And the sad little driver smiles smugly at the dent he's just left in the Ferrari's door. Or the mindless moron who gets some kind of kick out of running a key down the wing or across the boot or bonnet of the Aston Martin that someone else owns.

These are the same people who want to be what you are. They want to be successes and they are frustrated at their own inability, their lack of skill, knowledge and talent and their own failure to "become what you have done". Their irrational behaviour is jealousy, rage, anger and frustration all rolled into one and it shows itself in damage to successful people's property or is aired in spiteful verbal slander. It isn't acceptable, but it is almost inescapable.

Can anything ever be done to change the situation? When I was much younger, I set out in the world with a simple philosophy. I didn't want to change the world and I still don't. I just wanted to modify it a little in the bits that I interact, react and engage with, so that I could live in it comfortably, free from stress, aggravation and out and out confrontation. I now realise that isn't going to happen and certainly not if I

Live **BIG**. Think **LARGE**. Act **SENSIBLY**.
How to make a fortune - without losing your friends!

continue live to in England. Here, I will always be despised for my success, no matter how successful I become and however much I donate to charity and other worthy public causes.

That, it appears to me, is the price of success and the only way I can change that is to affect and influence the people that work with me, affiliate with me, trade with me and are influenced by me. It isn't much, but it is a start.

You can't change the world and only a few men or women that have been born ever could or have. All you can ever do is accept your place in the world, aware of both its beauty and its badness and make your way in the best way that you can. I don't want you to apologise for being successful to anyone. I am certainly never going to do that. I'm proud of what I've done, proud of who I am and what I've become and I'm proud of all that I've achieved. And I think you should always be proud of your success too. Never be shy of your success. There's no need to be arrogant or complacent about it either. But you did it, you achieved it and you should enjoy every minute of it and with quiet satisfaction you should celebrate it, every day. I do.

I sat once at a dinner table in Holland with a collection of very powerful business magnates. Some had more wealth than others and all had different levels of charm and ability at their chosen fields. But it was the richest idiot of all that provoked everyone's anger by declaring in a drunken haze that he "had enough money to buy anyone of us out, for cash, right there and then!" Needless to say the man's stock tumbled around the table and he was seen for what he was … an immature fool with neither breeding nor grace and whose time with his father's inheritance would soon run pretty thin as he squandered his money in dubious deals working with grovelling hangers on who were intent on bleeding him dry. It was a self-evident truth that *empty vessels do indeed make the most noise and that a fool and his money are soon parted.*

Yet I rubbed shoulders recently and got to know a man whose charm, elegance, grace and sophistication was the product of years and years of success. He looked nothing like his age and, quite remarkably, he was still encouraging his posse of eager listeners to do at least one of these things everyday - ski, run, swim, gym, cycle or power walk. This man has sold over $400 million USD-worth of products and services worldwide and built and sold over 21 companies making himself hugely wealthy. But you couldn't wish to meet or be in the company of nicer, kinder, gentler or wiser man.

Success hasn't spoiled him. In fact and he'll tell you himself it has made him a better person, better able to understand himself and the richness that life has to offer everyone who has eyes to see it and the wit and wisdom to grab it. And Ted Nicholas has repeatedly used his enormous gifts to help lots and lots of people, everywhere, often asking nothing in return and preferring to keep out of the spotlight and completely shunning the publicity. Aged just 29, Ted was voted one of the 50 best and most successful business people in America and was invited to the White House to meet the President of the United States!

Success is a gift that is not given lightly and we must all learn to accept it gracefully and use it wisely. Sure, you can't change the world, but through your success you can make life a lot better for a lot of people that you come into contact with. I know that I'd far rather be appreciated than hated, but I am not going to flinch whenever people hurl their spitefulness at my success.

You shouldn't either. You can't change the world and everywhere you go there will be people who will despise your success. You have to learn to live with it, be comfortable with it and if you can do that I have a strong hunch that you'll become better person because of it.

> *"Many of life's failures are people who did not realise how close they were to success when they gave up."*
> Thomas Edison, American inventor & businessman 1847-1931

Chapter 9

What shapes who you are?

"Any life, no matter how long and complex it may be, is made up of a single moment, the moment in which a man finds out, once and for all, who he is."

Pablo Neruda, Chilean writer and communist activist, 1904-1973

ADVERSITY. PLAIN, pure and simple. It's how you deal with the problems that surround you that will determine who you are and measure all that you can become. Everyone has issues every single day. All of us, great or small, rich or poor, intelligent or super intelligent, we all have a daily string of complications, demands and problems to deal with and try to resolve. Among all of that you have to try to find time to live your life, improve your skills, stretch your brain and keep up to date with the world's events and the relentless pace of change. Who ever said that living was easy?

Your childhood helps. If it was settled and stable and you felt loved and treasured then you have been given great gifts to begin with. Those gifts will be mightily important in helping to shape the adult you can become. I say "can become" deliberately because there are no guarantees. I've seen, as you have, kids that have had everything. They were treasured, loved, sported and celebrated throughout their childhoods. And then they promptly went and wrecked their lives on the rocks of desperation and the need to rebel and "be something

Live BIG. Think LARGE. Act SENSIBLY.
How to make a fortune - without losing your friends!

different". These people seem to want to spend their adulthood paying the price for a loving childhood and to me that just seems an odd way to want to live out the short time that each of us has here.

Then there are others who didn't have such a comfort trip. They didn't feel cherished and there wasn't a whole lot of love to go round. What those children got they took from wherever they could find it. They learned morality, ethics and honour from their friends, books, comics, films and occasionally school - if the school was any good and had something to offer. They learned love from other people. And they learned to build bridges all by themselves with just a few tools and a little knowledge. They became rugged individualists and often these are the people who do well in adulthood. There's a hunger about them and it's not just in a literal sense. They are hungry to prove themselves worthy in every way and it drives them to super achieve. If you know what it feels like to be hungry - and not just for food - then you do everything you can that is within your power and compass to never, ever go there again. That can be a massive motivator in the game of life.

It's not about proving yourself against the world as so many pretend intellectuals and overpaid psychoanalysts seem to think. It's about proving yourself against you. It's about knowing how good you are and how good you can become. And, if you've never had it, it's about finding out how good it really is when finally you achieve your goal, reach your ambition, or earn your dream.

But there isn't a man or woman on this planet of any age that has nothing left to learn. And it is never ever too late to try. What should I try? Get real! Take up painting or photography. Read your way through Dickens, Shakespeare or Hardy. Learn another language. Play a musical instrument. Try the piano, make something, sculpt, garden - the world is your oyster and everything in it is yours … if you want it. But like I've said, over and over again - life and success isn't going to come and find you. You have to get out there and find it! You must believe that it is never too late at any age to acquire new skills, new methodologies and new understanding. It is the only way to travel through this life or any other, but if you put up the shutters and close the door, then it's over, or as good as! So be prepared. Look life full in the face and hook up to all its challenges and your life will be the richer for it - and so will your pocket probably too!

Sensitivity matters too. You don't have to be rock-like and granite-faced to succeed. There's a time to be tough when you have to deal with unpleasant issues and discipline staff, or chew over disagreements with suppliers. But there's a time to recognise that a little softness can often work wonders, turning nagging doubts into positives, elevating people's belief in you and your business and creating a happier more purposeful atmosphere. And all you had to do was recognise someone else's suffering or deal with their concerns.

A boss I once worked for was particularly good at this. He was adept at getting to "know" the things that mattered most to the 20 or so people that worked for him. He got to know in a casual kind of way what made them tick, what made them happy and what kept them motivated. He knew his staff and he could see when they were bothered and each time he dealt with it, resolving their issues with whatever it took. For one guy, who had a gambling problem and was about to have his house repossessed, his boss stepped in, picked up the debt, paid off the mortgage arrears, got him counselling and turned the whole sticky problem into a longterm loan that was to be paid off in regular amounts from his salary. The boss's action gave the man his life back, but much more than that he had bought an employee's loyalty for life, showed his hand to his staff who all heard about it on the office grapevine and in one very simple action, a kindness to another human being, the boss had done something for which he could feel uniquely satisfied. It really doesn't take much to be human and to help others deal with their own weakness and folly.

Contrast that with another boss I once knew. He was a scheming, grasping, mean and, frankly, thoroughly nasty piece of work. He was all smiles, grace and charm to your face and pure evil behind your back. I mention him only to give balance to what I have so far written and my point is this - not everyone who has major wealth, or who has acquired obscene wealth, either understands it or knows how to use it. This man took delight in gobbling up the businesses of competitors that he had managed to break. Life was to him a cruel game of chess and the winner not only won but got to break all of the pieces and smash up the board as well. Cross him and he would go after you in any way that he could until he had finally rubbed your nose in the dirt. To my mind, life's rich bounty goes way, way beyond such meanness and I don't normally have time for brainless trolls, but I think this individual deserves to be immortalised in print as a lesson to all of us who would be "kings".

He took delight in telling everyone who would listen that he had managed to bankrupt a once-favoured supplier who had "crossed him". So much so, that on the day of the said "offender's" total demise, the day his house was repossessed and his possessions were turfed out onto the front lawn and

Live **BIG**. Think **LARGE**. Act **SENSIBLY**.
How to make a fortune - without losing your friends!

his wife and two small children stood weeping, the man who had caused all of this stood with his camcorder recording the whole sorry situation. Some time later, the poor guy who had lost everything took to drinking heavily and, one night while thoroughly drunk, got into his car and smashed it at speed into a motorway bridge leaving nothing but smoking wreckage and four shattered lives.

The man who had caused all of this was celebrated by some as a "fine fellow" and considered an upstanding citizen. He had chaired national charities, knew important people by name, moved in the finest circles and counted celebrities as friends. He was and remains one of the most worthless men I have ever known. Those who really knew him thoroughly hated him and yet he was good at weaselling his way into big contracts with massive companies and earning sizeable chunks of money. But for all his wealth and all of his contacts, for all his skills and undoubted abilities, what had this man's *Midas Touch* taught him? Nothing because he was too blind to see that the money actually matters much less than the people who actually help you to make it. Life is a people business and we all need to remember that and from time to time remind ourselves of that small and simple yet massively important fact.

And then there's realisation. Maturity in life often comes at a price, but what is maturity when you actually weigh it up? Maturity is a realisation. It is finally coming to terms with who you are and what makes you what you are. It is a realisation of what you can achieve and what you are capable of, but it is also a slow awakening of what you are not and the gradual dawning of what you cannot do. Maturity is about coming to terms with what you are not, which helps to steer you toward a better sense and proportion of who you are.

Maturity also gives you power, a power over yourself so that you can channel your energies, your drive and your focus into the things you do best which in turn helps and enables you to achieve impressive results. I like to think that I've gotten better both as a person and a businessman with each passing year. I've learned more about myself, understood more about the way life works and come to realise, with growing maturity, the certainty and meaning of what I'm doing. It isn't so much a spiritual journey as a simple celebration, a celebration of certainty because I now know what shapes me and where I am headed.

And you know it is funny in a strange kind of way the things that can influence, help, shape and drive you into becoming you. A few years back I happened upon ten things that I believe can help everyone to shape a better more rewarding, more certain and more fulfilling life and you'll never guess where I found them. It was in the Daily Express, an ordinary everyday tabloid newspaper that one day printed a strong message that I think everyone needs to hear. I have shared these Top Ten Tips for a Better Life with many people down the years and I can tell you for certain that it actually sits over the desk of a much-respected police sergeant who insists that every new recruit reads it, internalises it and acts upon it. For your pleasure here they are:

Ten things that might help you do everything better...

1. *Don't interrupt other people's sentences....*

People go to therapists because they feel no one is listening to them. Give friends, family and co-workers respect and listen to what they have to say. They'll be amazed and your relationships will benefit.

2. *Make peace with imperfection...*

Life is rarely as you want it to be. It's just one thing, after another. Always has been, always will be. The sooner you can accept that, the better.

3. *When you die your in tray won't be empty...*

People leave work depressed if they haven't done everything. Everyone has the same 1440 minutes in a day. Just do the best you can with them.

4. *Be the first to act loving or reach out...*

This is important. We're all stubborn. "I'm not going to be nice because they're not being nice to me." It's madness. Be first to start the process – you'll feel good and bring out the best in yourself and in others too.

5. *Ask yourself this – "Will this matter a year from now?"...*

Unless someone is extremely sick, terminally ill, or dead most of the things you're upset about now won't matter in an hour, let alone tomorrow.

6. *Be aware of snowball thinking...*

Don't blow things out of proportion. Dwell on an unimportant event and it quickly turns into a big deal and you don't realise it's happening ... until the consequences arrive.

7. *Let go of the idea that relaxed people can't be super-achievers...*

There is myth that unless you're mean, jumping on people, criticising everything you won't get on. A relaxed person has a calmer wisdom, access to greater common sense and sees solutions more easily. Try to show a little more tenderness in all that you do.

8.   *Always choose being kind over being right...*

People are obsessed with being right and proving it. Therefore, everyone else has to be wrong. If you want to be peaceful and happier, allow others to be right some of the time. It helps us all when we think about how others are feeling about what we do and say.

9.   *Every day, tell at least one person something you like or appreciate about them...*

You have to make this a habit. Turn all of your attention to what's right in your life, not what's wrong. Even if you don't receive a compliment in return you will still feel good and happier about who you are.

10.   *Live this day as if it were your last...*

... and treat your friends, co-workers, colleagues and contacts as if it might be their last too. It might well be... When you spend time with anyone, or talk with anyone, try to be nice – you'd really regret it if your last conversation with someone whose life was suddenly ended was spiteful, mean or nasty.

What a strange and wonderful journey life is! So many things shape who we are, but it's our knowledge of who we are that determines how we behave toward others and ultimately it's that knowledge that will shape our success.

"Live as if you were to die tomorrow. Learn as if you were to live forever."

Mahatma Gandhi, Indian political and spiritual leader, 1869-1948

Live **BIG**. Think **LARGE**. Act **SENSIBLY**.
How to make a fortune - without losing your friends!

Chapter 10

The power of choice

"There are always two choices, two paths to take. One is easy and that is its only reward."
Anonymous

YOU SHOULD never forget that you always have a choice and it's a power that you should try to exercise more often. Remember in class when you were much younger and you'd burst out laughing? The teacher would throw an outraged wobbly and ask you why you were laughing (somehow, it was always a serious moment in the lesson) and you'd say, "He made me, Sir!" or it was, "She made me, Miss!" It seemed to happen a lot less often with girls, as I remember. Maybe they just didn't have as much to laugh about.

Of course, you're older now and you know better. You also know that no one can actually physically make you laugh unless they are holding you down and tickling you in all the right places. You laughed back then because you chose to, not because someone made you. And that's the power of choice - you get to do something because you want to, not because someone forced you into doing something.

Choice is something that each of us and all of us forgets at one time or another. Forgetting provides a convenient excuse. It masks failure, reluctance, errors of judgement and a hundred other shortcomings. But choice is a powerful weapon in determining who we are, but also in helping us to decide all that we can become.

We all have a choice to make and it's a difficult one. Trouble is, we keep being forced to make that same choice time and time again. What choice is that? It's this: you can sit back and settle for what you've got and you'll get through life riding on whatever it gives you. You may be happy, I can't say, but if you sit back and settle for what you've got don't then point the finger of hate at the people who didn't sit back and settle because you don't have the right. You gave up that right when you sat back and just "let it all happen".

The other choice you've got is to take what you've already got and strike out for something better. You may succeed, I can't say and I sincerely hope that you do. But at the very least you will have exercised the enormous power of choice and earned the right to try to make something exciting, special and very different happen in your life. And what a feeling it is when something you do brings you the success you deserve!

I can't begin to tell you about the number of difficult choices that I have had to make to get where I have gotten myself to today. This book just isn't long enough! But I also know that I am not alone. All of the world's most successful people have made difficult choices along the way and all have had to make some tough decisions. That's life and that's what business is all about.

They tell me that supremely intelligent people have the most difficulty with making choices. Not being supremely intelligent I wouldn't know, but I think I can appreciate what the scientists and researchers are saying when they make such a telling statement. I think that intelligent people, quick people, sharp people, bright people and all of those of a similar kind (high IQs) have trouble with choices and decisions because they can "see the whole picture". They see the whole span of their actions and all of the possible range of consequences and outcomes and that's what freezes them and leads to monumental, often catastrophic indecision. For example, many lives were lost that could have been saved in the Titanic shipwreck if hesitancy, indecision and unbelievable arrogance could have been avoided in those who should have known better. But again, that's life and sadly it took 1500+ lost lives to give everyone 20:20 vision after the event.

I've seen really great and intelligent people baffled and bamboozled by choice. Should I do this, or should I do that? Buy this or buy that? Deal in this, or trade that? I've also watched others make huge decisions based on the spin of a fortune wheel or the simple toss of a coin! Myself, I've gone into situations having made my choices, unsure of the outcome, but aware of the possibilities for both failure and success. I've held fast when my heart has been racing, the blood pumping in my ears and the perspiration rolling freely down my spine. That happens when you stand up to talk to an audience of business people! It can be one of the most frightening choices you ever make. It is difficult, even when you're absolutely sure of your ground, sure of your content and know exactly what you need to say.

I can't tell you how to exercise the power of choice, but I want you to recognise its reality and never for one second underestimate its value. Remember in this game of chance called life it would take an extraordinary set of very unusual circumstances for anyone to be able to force you to do anything. The Gestapo could, hunger and thirst can, but in the main you get to choose without having to suffer the consequences of force.

It's easy to get lazy and let things slide. You see it all the time in the galaxy of global professional sports superstars. Paid obscene amounts of money (is there a footballer anywhere that justifies £130,000 a week?), they seem to forget what made them great. They stop doing those extra practices, stop putting in the effort in training, stop working in the matches and suddenly their "form" slides and they start to slip off the radar. It happens gradually at first, then it gathers momentum and suddenly they're gone, they're history in little more than an instant. They had a choice, for sure and, for the most part, they chose the easy option. When all of your creature comforts are taken care of, when all of your wants and needs are sorted and satisfied, you really don't have to work hard any more … do you?

Bad choice! A really bad choice. It's when you're at the top of your game that you have to work so much harder to make good, great and extraordinary things happen all of the time. That's when clever choices really do start to count. And clever choices can lengthen your playing career, whether you're starring in the boardroom or making a stellar name in sport.

But I'm getting ahead of myself a bit here. I make my own choices based pretty much on knowing the certainty of the outcome. I believe that most good gamblers do that. You take a given set of circumstances. You weigh up the possibilities, the options and the consequences. In business, you know what the break-even point of the choice you have made is likely to be. You know what revenue you need to make in order to cover the choice you have made. You've done the homework, the research and the groundwork and you can predict with reasonable certainty what might happen. And so, primed with information and business intelligence, you're 60-70% certain of success. Now that seems like a good gamble to me and it's a choice I am willing to make!

However, when it comes to staking millions on a roll of dice, a roulette wheel, or a thoroughbred racehorse, you can count me out! Without moralising, I don't see gambling as anything like a wise choice. At best, it can only ever be a 50:50 deal. In my life, I like a lot more certainty than that, especially about the choices that I make. And that's probably why I chose to make a career and my fortune in direct response and internet marketing. It is a truly fascinating area! Here is the "real science of choice".

More than that, you don't need masses of capital to get started. You can build your capital quickly from the very first brick that you ever lay. And, if you make the right choices, you can watch your capital grow substantially in a remarkably short space of time, as I have. What's direct response marketing? It's what Richard Branson and his Virgin brand has done since they started. And it's what made Anita Roddick famous with her chain of Body Shop franchises. Put simply, it's *directing* your product, service, solution or application right at the people who are most likely to buy. The more people you can find, the richer you'll become, provided you have something they want. And both Branson and Roddick gave the public what they wanted in spades and lorry loads.

Internet marketing is much the same thing. You're pitching products, services, solutions or applications to a global audience, not just a UK audience. And billions of people worldwide compared to 60+ UK million seems like sensible choice to me! All you have to do is come up with something that the public wants and get it out there. You offer the public informed choices and they make the decisions to buy. The certainty that I like is that you can do plenty of market research before you pitch anything to anyone, which will give you a fairly reliable indicator of what is likely to happen with the choice you have made. And you have the absolute evidence of results in sales and purchases. That's my kind of gamble! And it is fascinating. You've got low overheads, little need for expensive premises, virtually no storage costs, no standing stock, a skeleton of onsite staff and the lowest possible marketing and advertising expenditure. Find a crowd that's hungry for what you have to say or sell and much of what you make is pure profit. It is an exciting, fun and easy to manage business model and that's probably why I'm so delighted with the choice I made.

Perhaps I make everything sound too easy but I make no apology for that. I want you to let go of the side rail, come out bravely into the middle and swim to make your life better than it is now, or ever has been before. That's your choice and the power of that choice is in your hands. No one ever said you can't have what you want and, if they did, let me tell you - *they were wrong!*

The only person that will ever stand in your way ... is you. The only thing that stops you ... is you. The only opposition you will ever have ... is you. In fact, the only real competition you will ever in your life is with yourself! It's not about "other people". It's not even about "other companies". It's actually about you. It's going to be your vanity that makes you compete against other people and against other companies for that sacred number one slot … to be the best.

You don't have to top the Google listings. You don't have to be the outright market leader. You don't even have to be World Number One. You can make a very tidy living and a not inconsiderable fortune just be being number two, number three or even lower than that just by running your business along the lines of honesty, integrity and ethics without burning considerable energy and wasting huge resources to be the very best. Sometimes, it even pays to settle for second best, if only for a short while because the laws of business dynamics go some way toward proving that the very best always rises to the very top. Cream always does and if you are good enough, you will get there. Ask the Google boys - nowhere to everywhere in little more than the blinking of an eye!

Never forget that you have a choice and it's the way that you exercise the power of that choice that will always continue to pay you the richest dividends. Work out how to use it and make the power of choice work for you. That's winning … without gambling.

"It's choice - not chance - that determines your destiny."
Jean Nidetch, founder of Weight Watchers International

Chapter 11

Dealing with your demons!

"Only when we are no longer afraid do we begin to live."
Dorothy Thompson, celebrated American journalist, 1893-1961

WE ALL have them and let me tell you straightaway that no one is perfect. Well, perhaps Mother Theresa came close, but the rest of us are just bumbling along with our own inadequacies, trying to resolve them, eradicate them, temper them and just work hard to make them better. We're not trying to change the world, just adjust it a little so that we can live in it a lot more comfortably. Does that sound like you? It sure sounds a lot like me!

So, what is it that stops you from becoming the enormous success that you believe you deserve to be? If I asked you to write down your "demons" right now on a piece of paper, what would you write? Let me guess ... fear, lack of confidence, lack of self-belief, lack of knowledge, better competition, not enough resources, lack of respect, evil parents-in-law! Okay I threw the last one in just to add a little humour to these heavy proceedings, but maybe it's true - you might well have "evil outlaws" who are spiking your efforts to achieve phenomenal success! If so, you need to write me and together we'll hatch a plan...

But seriously, you have to deal with your demons and that

means starting out by knowing exactly what they are. I'm suspecting that you have a pretty good idea already. You may not have articulated them, even to yourself. You may not have given these ghostly shapes any real identity yet, but you know they are there, waiting, always waiting to jump out and surprise you and spike your success. They are, as J K Rowling, celebrated creator of the wizard Harry Potter put it, the Dementors, spectral shapes that swirl around you in the haze of another dimension that is locked somewhere inside your head. But these "swirling shapes", these Dementors, will suck the soul right out of your success … if you let them, or continue to let them. Now you're not a wizard and you don't have a wand (utterly brilliant books by the way! Well done, J. K!), but you can still whip those Dementors that are swirling inside your head.

I tackled the problem of fear earlier in this book so I'm not going to go over that one again save to repeat that it is the single most crippling demon (or Dementor) that you or anyone else will ever have to come to terms with. Fear stunts you. It makes you walk with a metaphorical stoop. It makes you do strange things to cover it up. Daft things like little white lies, or even big barefaced lies! And as you've no doubt already discovered, even the smallest lie carries enormous consequences. Fear puts barriers where there should be none. It brings "the walls" in closer and they crowd, stifle and choke you. You can't move because fear makes it impossible. And you did that. You allowed it to happen because you let the fear take over. Face it. Whatever it is and no matter how many forms it takes in your life, face that fear, tackle and conquer those demons and the "walls" that you have built and that are now closing you in will be shattered.

You'll be free and you'll be better able to cope because you trashed your fears.

Stuart Goldsmith in his excellent book *Seven Secrets of the Millionaires* has this to say about dealing with your demons on your way to accumulating fabulous wealth:

1. Face up to your fears.
2. Give in to the truth.
3. Be prepared to pay the price.
4. Know what you have to give up in order to succeed.

It is an excellent analysis. Fear you now know all about. It won't ever go away until you deal with it. Give in to the truth is as good a piece of advice as you'll ever get from anyone, anywhere, who has ever been successful. Too many people spend way too long fighting the obvious self-evident truths in their lives. It sucks up their soul and eats into their achievements. What good is a product, service or solution if nobody wants it? Walk away. Why waste time, money, effort, energy and resources on something that is failing or looks like a loser? You're no good at public speaking. So take courses and classes and learn to do it better! You're not a motivator. If you're a boss or any sort of leader you have to be. Period! So get hold of the knowledge you need to improve your skills and do it today! The truth is ... give in to whatever the truth is telling and you will always know what that is. No need to pretend.

I've also dealt with the issue of price throughout this book and it isn't just the ticket that is attached to the item. As I've said, repeatedly, success comes at a price. You have to recognise that price, accept its value and be prepared to pay it if you wish to succeed on a truly massive scale.

What do I mean? Being successful is not easy. There is little time for "normal" relaxation in the life of a busy and successful person. You're under pressure and you're driven to succeed so there's not a lot of time for TV, socialising, spectating and "fun" relaxation. But playboys and party girls manage to do it. Yes and they've already made their money or, more likely, spending someone else's - their father's usually footing the bill for their indulgent excesses!

If you're not already, you're going to become a driven person, driven to succeed. It will obsess you and it should if you are determined to do it properly and in the shortest time possible. And busy people bursting with ideas don't have a lot of time for playtime because success is an exhausting and enervating business! That said, I absolutely agree with Ted Nicholas that you do need an outlet that takes you away from the bump and grind of business. I cycle, run, swim and gym every week and I try to fit those physical activities in at different times of the day, no matter how busy my schedule. I get a great adrenalin surge from doing explosive sport in a recreational way (ie: I don't try to hammer myself to utter exhaustion!). Sport as a workout clears my mind, adds zest to my day and gives me loads of extra energy to cope with my demanding schedule. You really should try it. It will give you a whole new perspective on life and radically improve your ability to cope with anything that life can throw at you, as well as making you look better (body shape and skin tone) and feel better (psychologically and physiologically).

In business, you're inevitably going to take on too much and try to do too much. Then you'll worry in case you can't cope, or you end up letting people down. Funny thing is, no matter how much you've committed to, you always manage to get it done, even if sometimes it is only by a hair's breadth or a cat's whisker!

Your social life is also going down the pan. Sorry, but it is. You won't have time to be here, there and everywhere, wasting time in small talk and idle chitter-chatter when you could be using those hours to recuperate or to increase your chances of success still further. You need to be very careful here because you could end up losing your closest friends and everybody needs them, so try to keep them close. I've found that your good and loyal friends will appreciate the strain you'll be under and will try to be accommodating and make allowances for you, but most won't understand you. They chose the easy option and will never be able to understand or appreciate why anyone would want to work so hard to earn success. It won't stop them wanting to share liberally in your success when you finally arrive, by the way!

In fact, most people won't understand that you don't have a clue about reality TV, aren't interested in soaps, don't watch celebrity masterchef, haven't heard of the apprentice and still think that neighbours are people who live next door! That's odd behaviour, that is, but you will know about websites, blog boards, customer to sales ratios, cost per thousand and how to find, license, create, manufacture, distribute and sell products. All the things that are necessary to earn yourself a fabulous fortune.

Then comes the hate. Again, I have dealt with this in another chapter and I don't want to go over it, but those very same people who chose the easy life are the ones who are going to be most outraged by your success. "You were lucky!" "You didn't/don't deserve it!" "Someone must've helped you!" Like I've said, they'll forgive you everything, pretty much, except your success. So be prepared.

And when you've finally made it and got your millions, be prepared for the "second phase of possession". That pretty much covers everybody who somehow and quite mistakenly seems to think they have a right to your money. You'll have solicitations for donations by the ton from just about every worthy and worthwhile institution and charity that has ever been invented or created. You'll receive letters and emails for help and assistance from everywhere you can imagine and some from places you couldn't possibly imagine. It will be a full time job just to deal with all of the plea-bargaining you're going to receive. But that's the lighter side of success and when you've got lots you can afford to be generous to worthy causes and things that are closest to you heart.

Stuart's last point, Point No. 4: *Know what you have to give up in order to succeed* is right on the money. It takes a lot out of you to succeed and it takes a lot from you to succeed. But first and foremost, you have to face your demons - whatever they are - and deal with them. And communication is key to enabling you to do this. Talk things through, with your partner, your business partners, associates, friends and colleagues. Get answers, assess opinions and then make decisions, after you have evaluated all of the available evidence. Don't be rash. Learn to be methodical and master the art of identifying the issues. Put a name to things. Don't just allow them to swirl about in the ether of your head, or fester in the reality of your business. If there's an issue, deal with it straightaway. In the end you'll be glad that you did. And learn, learn, learn! Challenge yourself. Challenge others. Know what you need to know and find the sources that can satisfy your insatiable curiosity - the need to know that drives and powers your business.

When you've worked out what it is that actually stops you from being the success you deserve you can then take the steps that are necessary to create the success that you want to see. It's not only easy - it is inspirationally exciting!

"Death is not the greatest loss in life. The greatest loss is what dies inside us while we live."

Norman Cousins, American essayist, 1912-1990

Live **BIG.** Think **LARGE.** Act **SENSIBLY.**
How to make a fortune - without losing your friends!

Chapter 12

Good rules to great housekeeping

"The important thing is this: to be able at any moment to sacrifice what we are for what we can become."
Charles du Bos, French critic of literature, 1882-1939

SLOPPY PEOPLE don't succeed - that's not an assumption, it's a fact. Success on a truly gigantic scale takes great housekeeping and that requires rules and orderliness, a tidy mind and an incredible focus. If you've got those qualities safely in your locker then you're ready for the big league.

There are three things that I consider to be essential in your make up if you are to succeed big style and they are:

1.   Only ever listen to the right people.
2.   Be resourceful and determined.
3.   Never, ever give up.

Case in point, a good business friend of mine recently faced a quandary and was mired in indecision. She didn't know what do and needed advice. So, who did she ask for advice? Her dentist! Now I can't think of a professional person who is less qualified to give considered business advice than someone who has no experience of the business you're in! Why would you do that and worse still, why would you listen? But people do it all the time, even immensely successful people that I know. Their first ally in a crisis or quandary is their wife or husband, or their partner. Now I'm not decrying that, provided the person you're consulting has the experience necessary to give you considered advice. But if they don't, all that you're most likely to hear is just what you want to hear, when what you really need is impartial, expert advice that can help you to reach a rational and well-considered decision.

That said, in my early business career, I sat in front of a "business expert" in plush offices, with delightful furniture and a very ordered filing and inter-office communications structure. I'd driven a long way to hear this man dispense his wisdom about how he could help my business, help me to make the "right connections" and even put me in touch with the right partners and affiliate organisations. All I heard when I got there was irrelevant rubbish. He didn't have a clue about me, my business, or how best to help me, but there he was, a man professing to be an expert. He may have been an expert, but at what I have no idea! I have since come across many such rogues, both in print, online and at some seminars that I've attended. For me, "expert" has become a word that has acquired some very sinister overtones. And that's why you'll never hear me calling myself an expert. I'm not an expert. I'm just someone who has acquired some of the gems of knowledge about how life works and how the business world can be made to deliver all of its riches and that is what I'm sharing with you as I write this book.

What I'm trying to say here is what I've said throughout the book - you have to know where to find the answers and you must leave no stone unturned, no file unopened, no area unexplored and no avenue untrodden as you search to find the answers. The answers won't ever come and find you. They never do.

Make it a rule of thumb that from now on you will only ever take advice from correctly qualified people. I think you'll find that your life and your business runs better for that one small simple decision. You might also find that your personal and inter-personal relationships run a lot smoother and are a lot less stressful too.

Another thing you can do right now is stop worrying. There are things you can change and things you can't and from long experience I can tell you that worrying about it won't alter the outcome much, if at all. You're just wasting your time, your effort, your energy and your sweetness and if you want to race yourself into an early grave then worrying about things is I'm sure one of the fastest ways to do it! Worrying makes no sense. It elevates your blood pressure - one of the biggest causes of heart attacks in the western world, makes you lose sleep and it definitely accelerates the ageing process with a criss-crossing of frown lines etched ever deeper into your face. And what will you have really changed? Nothing. Things run their course, that's the natural order of things and you worrying about it won't help drive the issue any further forward, or resolve it any quicker.

What is worry anyway but a state of hyper anxiety that is associated with procuring an outcome that you so desperately want to see. Life doesn't work that way and the more energy you expend in the negative (worrying) the less energy you have to spend on the positive side of your business (management, direction, control and exploring new opportunities). Worrying is damaging to your psyche and it impairs your ability to exert a positive influence. Ditch it and ditch the "ne'er do gooders" too!

You don't need negative people in your life. Sure you can't pay your way with optimism and you can't run a business on happiness alone, but positive, happy and cheerful people will radically influence business performance and make interaction easier to achieve across every level of your operation or organisation. Suppliers, traders, clients, associates and customers will hear happiness in the way the phone is answered and the speed with which their requests are processed and progressed. Research has proven time and again that happy people work harder and create an atmosphere of encouragement, enthusiasm and positive creativity.

Don't listen to people who want to tell you that "you can't". They'll always be there, ready, eager and willing to tell you why you'll fail. It's a story they know so well because they are starring in it themselves! As Bob Proctor writes in his book *You Were Born Rich, "Opinions are the cheapest commodity on earth and everybody is keen to give them away."* And that just about sums it. People will always want to put you down, especially if you're successful and if they have an opinion to offer (and most people do!) it is usually in the negative. It's about what you cannot do and cannot achieve, not what you can and will. You see, success and successful people frighten most people. They do things that most people don't, have an abundance of energy and are positive firecrackers of drive and enthusiasm. If that sounds like you, then you are everything that most people are not.

Similarly with the news, the papers, the press and the media. So much of what passes for news is about failure! It concentrates on the negative aspects of life and gives little airspace, credence or column inches to life's many successes. If you listen to the news, you wouldn't move or do anything because the signs of doom are all around us waiting to gobble us all up! You only have to listen to the weather broadcasts when we, here in the UK, have a few inches of snow! It's all don't, don't, don't and if you do, well you take your life in your own hands. Cripes, there are countries that get through huge snowfalls for months on end that don't behave like the British at the very first glimpse of snow. I'm not disputing that snow is a hazard and it can be life threatening, but please let's keep a sense of proportion about what it is and what it can do. Life goes on, whether it snows or not!

And it can be severely depressing and very disruptive to constantly read gloomy forecasts, downbeat and cynical business reports. Funny how, even in times of economic desperation, good companies launch, get off the ground, survive and create a name for themselves and completely contradict the doom-mongers in the process. If Google had followed logic and read all the reports about a saturated market, a dot com downturn, a dollar slide and all of the other good stuff that the press peddles out and wallows in they never would have given it a shot. Not very long ago Marks & Spencer shares were being traded for pennies. These were the shares no one wanted because the company was about to disappear. The grand old lady of British commerce was doomed, so the press and papers would have you believe. Look it at now. It has re-established itself as one of the country's top performing shares despite a welter of negative press and the imprudent and hasty comments of industry analysts. Yep, you really can't always count on the knowledge and insight of the experts and if you backed Marks & Spencer when they were in a tight corner, you're certainly laughing now.

As I see it, there are just four key stages to phenomenal financial success. You must:

1. Become absolutely debt-free.
2. Attain financial independence.
3. Amass considerable wealth.
4. Achieve your own personal goals.

Those are your targets on the road to riches. Get rid of the mortgage completely. It is drain on your pocket that you don't need. Forget the tax relief. That doesn't make any sense. Just get rid of the albatross that hangs round your neck and buy back those years of your life! Then put the money you've saved to good and better use on the road to financial independence. Shed the credit cards, pay off all the loans, clear the decks and start your own business(es) and watch as your wealth accumulates. As your wealth grows and your confidence soars and as your knowledge grows and your experience develops you'll see the opportunities unfold as a huge number of new avenues present themselves. Then your personal wealth will really take off and, one by one, you can tick off all of those personal lifetime goals that you have set yourself. Once you've reached the pinnacle, whatever your heart desires and whatever you have set your heart upon is yours for the taking. And it all starts with good housekeeping for that is your pathway to immense success.

Everyone has problems, that's a given, but the biggest

obstacle that you have to deal with to succeed is yourself! Yes, it's you. You are the biggest single threat to your own success.

People fail because they plan to fail. Turn that around and what it actually says is you will succeed if you plan to succeed! That is what I mean about good housekeeping and that is how simple success can be.

Many, if not most of the people I meet, want it all too easy. They EXPECT it to be child's play easy to make a fortune because someone once told them it would be. There's a fire. Go on then, stick your head in it. Well, you wouldn't would you because you know the consequences and, after all, only a fool would do something so stupid. Yet people "invest" in scams and risky businesses every day and it's a lot like sticking your head in a fire. But people do it all the same because they want that dream key that gives them pots and pots of money on a plate.

Unfortunately, the real world just doesn't work that way. Not in the beginning and not, as far as I know, for anyone that I've ever met.

If you want it you have to work at making your business a success, then it comes a lot more easily. But it is never easy in the beginning, not for anyone.

The important thing is … **never, ever give up!**

You've got to be resourceful, become proactive, think about things, challenge everything and do things. Research your markets, analyse your opportunities, assess what is possible, evaluate what is predictable and, once in a while, shoot for the moon and aim for the impossible!

You've got to be willing to work to make your business(es) work, but you've also got to be ready to make mistakes - and learn from them.

If you don't know the answers and you're struggling (and from time to time we all do) then find someone who does have the answers. Don't just sit there and watch as the hours slip away. Be resourceful, change things, look for answers and ask for help.

Problems are part of life and you can't solve all of them, but as an entrepreneur you have to learn to deal with them and solve the ones you can.

Your success in business and as a businessman is all about the attitude and approach that you bring to the table. It really is up to you and, while there are no free gifts, there is plenty of free money that you can make - if you only know where to look.

Here and now, I'm going to give you the psychology that I use to tackle my own problems. This is the formula that has kept me sane and surging forward. Oh and it's put a lot of money in my pocket, so I know that it works.

1. Why did this become a problem? Whatever it is, see it for what it is, identify it, look for explanations, find reasons and use the answers to drive you forward.

Simply apply logic to the problem to get to the cause(s) and then construct a resolution based on answers to your own questions.

I've found that this kind of interrogative process works for every kind of problem that business ever throws up at you. What was the cause and how can you fix it?

Stay calm, at all times, stay focused, peel back the layers one by one and, by degrees, you will be able to think your way to a resolution. Problem solving really can be that easy.

2. How have others solved these problems? In business, you're never alone and somewhere, for sure, some other entrepreneur has faced down the same issues and encountered the same problems that you are trying to tackle. How did they deal with them?

Go to online forums related to your business area and there you'll probably find the answers. Post your query and you'll find that lots of people are eager to give you help and guidance, analysis and advice.

There are hundreds of online resources available to help you. Some are great, some are bad and some are plain awful but if you dig around long enough you'll get to find the ones that work best for you, as well as those that are best avoided altogether.

Don't ever think it can't be done. Instead, find a way to prove that it can be done! That is how you succeed and all it takes is a positive mental attitude. Too often I hear "can't", "don't" and "won't". Those are the people that are destined to fail because they 'can't do this' and 'don't ever do that' and that 'won't ever work'.

Try this instead: *can, will and do! You can achieve this, you will try that and that's what you are going to do!* From somewhere, you have to find a positive mental attitude that will take you to all of your dreams and if you haven't already got a good healthy dose of optimism then it's time you bought some, found or, yes, even stole some. (But only if you have to!)

Read self-help manuals - there are tons around. Listen to the CDs produced by skilled personal motivators. Go to courses, take classes - do whatever you have to do to acquire a positive frame of mind that powers you out of the blocks every single day. The force that makes you a tough (but always fair) competitor and a determined individual who is always a pleasure to deal with, but who is always very focused and totally committed to what you have to do.

Success is all about you and your attitude. It is the power of positive thinking that gives you the self-belief you need to get out there and conquer the world - your world, however big you want that personal world of yours to be.

3. Be resourceful. Don't just sit there waiting for "good things" to happen. Chances are that they won't! In fact, they won't ever! Good things, great things and wonderful things happen because somebody made them happen. In your business, in your life - that person is you!

There's nothing that can't be tackled, nothing that can't be resolved and nothing that can't be made to work if you analyse it and think it through. Here's the issue, this is the problem, now how do I solve it? Trust me, however bleak it may appear at the outset, there is always a way. Always. You just have to find it, that's all.

Who can you call? Where can you look? What do you need and who has it? My favourite resource is the internet - it has the answer to virtually everything you'll ever need, somewhere. It just may take a while to find it, but it's there.

Develop the habit of being resourceful and "getting things done" and you'll soon find it becomes second nature. You'll find yourself tackling more and more, with even greater relish and enthusiasm than ever before. You're rejuvenated and ready and well on the way to the door of success.

4. Travel with an open mind. In business as in life, you should always try to 'keep the door open' and you don't have to leave your desk to travel anywhere. Just open your mind and you're away. Don't shut your mind to influences and experiences because you never know where the next tidal wave of consumer passion is going to come from or strike next.

Friends of mine travel with their eyes wide shut and all you ever hear is: "I wish I'd thought of that!" They probably could have, but most likely they "couldn't be bothered". It's your future and you owe it to yourself to make a huge effort to be receptive to all kinds of influences. That way, you can recognise opportunities as they unfold and if you can get in at the start of something then that is often where all the real profit is to be made.

5. I've read that - I know that. Maybe you have, but did you internalise it? Did you make it part of your daily practice? Too many people pass up on too many gems of information. They read it, remember it for a short while and then something else interrupts and it gets pushed out of their consciousness. They forget what they have learned, even though at the time, it was the most valuable thing they knew!

Keep going back to the basics and keep on re-reading the best self-help, motivational philosophy books that you've found because that is what will make you a "truly great player" in any league, anywhere. It's all about repetition and practice and most definitely about knowledge and action!

Read it, know it, but always make sure you practice and action it.

6. Find good people. I can't emphasise this enough. Surround yourself with good people, the very people that can help you to get to your dreams. Such people are like cut and polished diamonds - they sparkle with fire and energetic enthusiasm for what they do, but like diamonds they have so many surfaces. They carry such knowledge and experience that they are truly gems. But treat them well always.

7. Never stop opening doors. I've said it already but it needs repeating: *there is no one who has nothing left to learn.* No one. Things change all of the time. What worked last week, last month or last year may not work at all this week. That's just how life is. But that's not a problem. The problem is when you stop learning, stop trying and stop opening doors.

Feed your mind, fire up your curiosity, get to know, want to know, prompt, probe and stretch your mind, all of the time and in every way you can think of.

That's the creative challenge that's on the table - to be as good as you can possibly become. That means opening every door you come across. Some are just full of garbage but most you'll find are not and it's amazing what you can learn and take away whenever you just open the door and take a look.

8. Listen. It's a wise old truism but it needs to be said: *People who learn most listen hardest!* And there are many ways to hear. 'Listen' to what life and the business markets are telling you - it can make you a fortune and it can stop you losing one! But you don't need to do that with your ears - you 'listen' with intelligence from the information you receive, see and read.

Grab everything that can help you sharpen your business brain and marketing skills because *listening makes things happen.*

Go to seminars, run your business and motivation CDs and DVDs again and again, talk frequently to your business associates and other entrepreneurs. Listen closely to what they have to say but, above all, listen to your customers. Remember, it's not about you - it's about *them* and you have to learn to listen intensely to what they are telling you if you are to succeed in the ways you've been dreaming about.

As Sam Walton, founder of Wal-Mart, once put it:

> *"There is only one boss. The customer. And he can fire everybody in the company from the chairman on down, simply by spending his money elsewhere."*

The customer is your boss too and you must listen to what they are telling you. Your fortune and your future depend on it.

9. Ask. You will surely fail if you don't learn to do this. You can't know everything and you can't do everything and sometimes you just get stuck. Eat a bit of humble pie and ask somebody that is likely to know or who you think can help you to find the answer or solve the problem.

Ask nicely and you'll find most people are only too willing to help you. Even the most respected of today's marketers will help you, if you can get to them, but the point is that someone, somewhere, knows the answer and that answer can keep you on track and very likely help keep your business intact.

Never be afraid to ask for help. I never have and I am proud to number among my personal friends and business associates some of the world's most respected marketers and best business brains.

10. Remember. It's easy to forget. Easy to forget what got you started, easy to forget what you are trying to do and easy to forget the principles of good business and great customer care. It's easy to forget everything - so write it all down!

If you've got a great memory you can carry a lot of things in your head. Most of us haven't so make lists of all that you've got to do each day and tick them off one by one as you accomplish them. Don't worry - you won't be able to do everything on your list, every day. Trust me, even when you die your in tray is still going to be full, but don't beat yourself up about it. Think positively and be satisfied by what you have accomplished this day, today and be glad that there may well be a tomorrow.

If I could share two tips with you it would be these: firstly, remember to thank people sincerely for the help they've given you and, secondly, always over deliver - it impresses your customers in ways that make them remember you and it keeps them coming back to you for more.

Being in business is fun and it should be, all of the time. You should look forward to the *pleasure every day brings* and not get hung up about the pressure being in business brings. The pressure is a by-product of the tremendous opportunity for success you hold in your hands. You really do have the keys to the riches of the kingdom - your kingdom - and it is entirely up to you how you use them. No one can turn the lock for you. All we can ever do is get you to the door and the rest is up to you. From here, you write your own story.

"You have to learn the rules of the game. And then you have to play better than anyone else."
Albert Einstein, 1879-1955

Chapter 13

Success never stops...

"Success is never ending: failure is never final. It's courage that counts."

George F Tilton, American sports psychologist

THE FUNNY thing is that once it starts, success just doesn't stop. Many, many of the world's best entrepreneurs have said the same thing in lots of different ways, but what it boils down to is this: *the harder you try, the luckier you get!*

Put simply, what that means is that the harder you try the more doors open to you, creating more opportunities and even greater levels of success. Luck? Yes, I guess luck has something to do with it, but it's more about you steering your own course successfully than it is about luck blowing the wind in your sails to ship you safely into harbour. That's pretty much what most people mean when they say: *You make your own luck.* You do. You absolutely do.

For my own part, the harder I've tried, the luckier I've been. By that, I mean that more doors have opened because I've met the right sort of people that I can associate with and they have presented other opportunities or made introductions that have led to affiliate relationships and complementary deals.

And as I've motored through life (sorry, but I don't have time to meander!), I've learned the lessons it has served up. I've gathered experience, I've increased my intelligence and expanded my knowledge and I've come to learn what works and what doesn't. I've developed a "good nose" for success and a healthy feel about "no-goes" and possible disasters. You'll do that too and the more you learn and experience, the easier it all becomes to find those big winners. You'll also find a few losers too. Everyone does. But it is never the loss that's the problem. It is how you deal with the consequences that is the real problem.

A few too many people that I've met let the failure hang like as lead weight around their necks. It distresses them and, if you allow it, a failure can destroy you too. So you made a relatively poor decision. What did it really cost you? A little money, that's all. Live with it. Learn from it. You won't make the same mistake again, now will you? Not unless you're seriously stupid and having read this far, I'm guessing that you're not!

I once travelled in the chauffeured car of a printer that I used to use. He wanted me to accompany him to make a presentation to a very important client that he was desperately trying to impress and from whom he hoped to secure a substantial contract. It was quite a long journey and on the way the printer fielded a phone call from a distressed customer. The printer had specially designed and printed 250,000 window envelopes bearing the phrase *The world is waiting* ... to the front and the printer's own PO Box return address on the reverse flap. The client had rejected them because the window was in the "wrong place" and she "couldn't possibly use them" and the printer would have to reprint and remake at his own cost.

Unfazed, the printer took the call, answered with appropriate and charming humility and, after closing the conversation flipped his phone shut and smiled at me. He stood to lose several thousand pounds on the strength of that one phone call, but within a matter of minutes, he was on the phone to another customer and with a style, the like of which I have rarely seen before or since, he had convinced the new customer to buy the 250,000 envelopes for which, he the printer would print 250,000 personalised letters onto letter headings that were stock items "held" for this particular client and charge him only for use of the PO Box, the envelopes and the printing of the letterheads.

In effect, the printer, from a position of having to make a loss on 250,000 envelopes, walked away from the new deal with a tidy profit. He'd "sold" the envelopes, was able to charge for the print on 250,000 letters and was also charging the new client for using his postal box. Disaster avoided, profit made! And the profit he was about to make would more than make up for the "loss" of having to redesign and reprint the window envelopes for his original client ... who was also paying for letters to be printed as well as the use of the printer's postal box.

The whole deal was completed in less than fifteen minutes and the loss he was about to suffer disappeared in the profit he was about to make from servicing two customer's needs. Brilliant. A brilliant piece of lateral thinking done on the spot and a clever example of how you can rescue a seemingly impossible situation if you "simply know who to call".

Lucky? Perhaps lucky enough to know the right people in exactly the right chain to turn a sticky situation around, but there was nothing at all lucky about the printer making the "right connections". And his ability to do that, simply and swiftly, averted a potentially costly disaster for his company. As I've said throughout this book ... *"only connect".*

Business and success is very much about making all those vital connections. You can't make it on your own. Few people ever do. You need a team, you need good people to support, assist, help and guide you. You need good bankers, good accountants, good bookkeepers and back office people and probably a reputable legal team in your corner too. You need backup, associates, affiliates and trading partners, but above all, you need customers - and you need lots of 'em!

And that has really been the whole point of this book. I've tried to share with you my philosophy of what it takes to be a winner and a qualified success. Don't for a moment assume that those two are one and the same thing. They aren't. You can win big, but still be a failure in the drive to reach your dreams and achieve your goals. Winning is only part of the equation. What you really want is consistent success and that is what will make you a longterm winner.

But when we talk about wealth, what are we really talking about? I read somewhere recently that unless you have £3 million then you're not wealthy at all. I personally know the marketing man that actually wrote that statement and I have to take serious issue with the sentiment because I simply don't believe it to be true.

This is your dream and you must decide - entirely for yourself - what equates to success ... for you and for you alone. If you're completely debt-free and you're sitting on

£30,000 then I think you're probably sitting pretty ... for the moment. Obviously, you can't stay there and hang on in that position because your outgoings and expenses will soon gobble that tidy little sum up. Start your own business and £30,000 will hardly stretch anywhere, but that's another story and not the point and purpose of this book.

If I could hand you a few things that I think really are important in your quest for success and the pursuit of immense wealth, it would be these:

1. Get yourself debt-free (and yes dump the mortgage, lock, stock and barrel!) as quickly as you can.

2. Work for yourself and start your own business(es) as soon as you can.

3. Surround yourself with good people. Find them and hold onto them. They are the rivets that will most definitely hold everything together for you.

4. Keep an open mind on everything and about everything.

5. Challenge yourself in every way you can possibly imagine. Challenge your intellect, develop your inquisitiveness and get into the habit of stimulating your mind every single day. Want to know and be madly curious. Read everything that matters. Go to seminars. Take courses. Read books. Develop the instinct of a good businessman and a capable entrepreneur and you are half way toward writing the kind of future that you believe you deserve.

6. Find your customers! The world is a very big place and the internet has put all of it on your doorstep. There are huge opportunities here and vast profits waiting to be collected for entrepreneurs with vision, clarity of thinking, good products and solutions offered at fair prices and backed by great service.

7. Believe in yourself. If you don't believe in you, how can you expect others to buy into your brand? You need to acquire the air of quiet confidence. There's no need to be brash, arrogant, loud, aggressive or objectionable. I've seen great bosses achieve wonderful things with just a quiet word here, or a little praise there and I've seen tub-thumpers turn a winning company into a mass walk out!

8. Never give up or give in! What you do, how you act and who you are can easily become a 'cycle of repetition' - if you allow it. Fail once, give up and walk away and the chances are that when the same scenario presents itself again, as it surely will, you'll repeat the same cycle in just the same way - you'll give up, give in and walk away. That's the 'cycle of repetition' and if you look back over your past you can probably recognise it in your past. That's not to say you blindly stick with what patently isn't working. You have to pick your winners and a wise man knows when to walk away. But too many people give up too early and walk away leaving all the money on the table ... for someone else to collect.

9. Learn to work with others. Now this is important. Too many people that I've seen can't do this. As much as anything, that's what stops their growth and prevents them from reaching all of their dreams. The simple truth is that it is a very rare person that can actually make it big all on his or her own. Most people need the help of others - yes, even George Soros - the international currency speculator and Warren Buffet, American investor and businessman - the second richest man on the planet (after Microsoft founder, Bill Gates) and certainly the world's greatest giver to worthy causes (estimated current net worth around US$46 billion). You've got to learn to "walk with everybody" if you're really going to go somewhere, *"even the dull and ignorant ... for they too have their story."* (Max Ehrmann, Desiderata)

10. Live BIG. Think LARGE. Act SENSIBLY. That's the title of this book and I hope that, as you've turned the pages, a lot of things have started to make a lot of sense and begin to add up. The future is there, if you want it. It's waiting for you to make it happen and make it work and it will deliver all that you want and you get to choose how and when that will happen. It really is all up to you.

As I've said, once you get started the success never stops. New waves keep rolling and every new wave brings new opportunities for you to consider, presenting fresh challenges that open entirely new doors. And every day is exciting because you're in command and you have control. You're steering yourself toward your dreams and all of the success you had planned out for yourself. You call the tune and you decide what's good, bad and acceptable.

And to my mind there is no finer feeling to be had than a successful entrepreneur or businessperson who is sure of themselves, sure of their ground and certain of the future.

This is your time, it's your future and now it's time you took control.

"You must be resolutely determined that whatever you do shall always be the best of which you are capable."
Charles E. Popplestone, American business psychologist, author of "Every Man A Winner", 1936

Live BIG. Think LARGE. Act SENSIBLY.
How to make a fortune - without losing your friends!

Chapter 14

Questions that I'd like answered!

THERE ARE many things that baffle, amaze and astound me and so many books like this one that end with a chapter that exhorts you to do this, consider that, apply this and learn that. So I thought I'd do something a little different.

There are so many things that I can't explain and some, I suspect, that can't even be answered, so I thought I'd call up and contact a few of my very closest business friends, partners, suppliers and associates and try to get a handle on what has been and is still bugging them!

Here's what they said. Some if it is serious, some of it is semi-serious, some of it I hope will make you smile and, who knows, some of it might even make you think a little. But if you've got any answers, or you want to air your opinion, you are welcome to email me here at nick@nick-james.com. Who knows? Perhaps we can meet on "common ground" and find some real answers!

Q. Where do all the junk emails and undelivered messages that are never returned actually go?

They (who are "they"?) estimate that roughly 62 billion (BILLION!) email messages are sent every day. That's an awful lot of communication and I wonder just how much of it is wasted and never gets to go anywhere, let alone where it's intended! So what happens to it? It "floats" off into cyberspace and probably there, at the very edge of the galaxy, all of this knowledge and (pretty much) worthless communication may be coagulating and is being compressed, compounded and consolidated into a … a cyber life form, another planet, a meteor that will turn tail and streak back to the earth ready and armed to obliterate us all in a compressed form of uselessness! Now this doesn't keep me awake at night but I like to think that maybe, just maybe, life is less linear and logical than any of just can see or predict. And anyway, it's a lot of fun letting your mind have free rein, once in a while, don't you think?

Q. What is an itch and why do they always strike when your hands are full and you can't do anything about it?

On average, the human body is covered by 2 square metres of skin. It's the only organ constantly exposed to irritation and with the skin coming into contact with so many things daily, you're bound to get an itch or two. Itching (pruritus), starts with an external stimuli sitting on your skin. As soon as we feel an itch, our natural response is to scratch the spot of the itch to remove the irritant as soon as possible. That satisfies the brain's panic (it sees the itch as a potential danger, a bug bite or similar and prepares to "defend" itself) and we can go on our way … unless of course, your hands are full. Then the itch assumes full on aggravation ... and it always happens at just the wrong time! Life somehow always gets in the way when you're concentrating on other things!

Q. We share 98% of our DNA with chimpanzees so, is it likely that we will soon meet another type of animal in the boardroom and, if so, when?

Animals in the boardroom, now that is interesting! They say that we share 98% of what makes us human with chimpanzees, so I'm wondering just when our hairy friends will assume dynamic human proportions, don the shirt, tie and suit and find themselves sat at the head of global corporations? Come to think of it, some of them probably already are! We just haven't noticed it yet and the changes have been too subtle for us to realise. Perhaps the next time you're in the boardroom you could just check all-round for a full set of opposing thumbs...

Q. Does no really ever mean no - ever?

How many times have you said no and really meant to say yes? I can't begin to count the number of times I do it! Sometimes it's just easy to say no then it won't engage you in a lengthy, longwinded or embarrassing justification. But no is a word we use often with ill-considered caution and, for two small letters, no is a massive negative. Maybe we should all try a bit harder to use no better. That way, we can open the door to other possibilities and stop missing out on so many. Maybe is a word, it seems to me, that keeps more doors open and multiples the possibilities than a flat, straight no ever can. But it's a just a thought to make you think!

Q. At what point does a business actually achieve its critical mass?

I guess that point is reached when you just can't do, manage and control every aspect of your operation or organisation. When there's just too much to do, or too many orders to fulfil then clearly you need help and probably a team of people to help you administer all that the business now needs. Trouble is, it's a quantum leap from a tightly run, tightly knit operation with a handful of people to a major player with 15, 30, 50 and more, premises, inventory and a whole raft of other issues that you, or someone, will have to deal with.

There is of course a trade off too in that, after expansion, it's hard for you to be looking for new avenues and different opportunities. Expansion consumes your energies and if it is too rapid without careful control it can prove ruinous. Remember Hutchison's Rabbit mobile phone technology from Whampoa? No, I don't remember much about it either, but blind ambition, driven by errant belief in what the public wanted and a dodgy technology platform and hey, you've got yourself a spectacular failure.

The important thing is to develop your business with your exit strategy in mind. When do you want to leave? How do you want to leave? What should the business have given you and what can it do for you, after you leave it?

Q. What happens when all the hard drives fail?

Here we are in this digital age, becoming increasingly dependent on technology. Everything we do is being stored somewhere on a server and books, the great literature of our lives, are also being transposed to disk and electronic storage. Soon, nothing will exist in hard copy format. It will only exist digitally on a hard disk somewhere ... and if catastrophe were ever to strike and every hard drive be erased the world's knowledge, certainly from this point forward, would be lost ... forever because no one has a hard copy of anything, any more. Makes you think, doesn't it, about where we're heading with the brave new world of digital technology and electronic utility?

Q. How can I keep my friends?

The more successful you become, the harder it becomes to hold onto your friends because time is always at a premium for you and so contact even with those friends that are closest to you becomes increasingly infrequent. Recognise that and you can do something about it, if you want to. But if you want my honest advice, never ever employ your friends and family in your business, not if you want to keep your sanity ... and keep your friends!

I sincerely hope you've enjoyed reading my book and feel you've got something positive and worthwhile out of it. How you take it forward from here is entirely up to you, but these are the lessons and observations that I have put into daily practice to get me well on the way to achieving all of my dreams.

Time waits for no one and success will never come and find you. In the end, you write your own dream, but there's no point in repeating everyone's previous mistakes.

I'd like to think we'll meet again at some future point, somewhere far down the road to your own success. Stay lucky, be happy, but above all, enjoy your journey.

Chapter 15

Your road to riches starts here...

YOU'VE READ everything and now you're ready to get started. You're pumped up and eager, but where do you begin?

My own site www.Nick-James.com can offer you a great starting point that can help steer you toward the many things you are going to need.

Here you'll find products that you can use, licenses you can buy, offers, views, hints, tips and all-round guidance on good business practice. There are other ebooks you can buy along with techniques and tools that will put you in touch with brilliant marketers and superskilled entrepreneurs who can help you to make sense of what you are doing.

And there are some of the best resources you could ever find to help you get where you wish to go. Writers, designers, thinkers, courses, manuals, books and access to an immensely valuable network of contacts - people who have already done what you are trying to do, or do better and more successfully than you ever have before reading this book.

Join my community and you'll regularly receive updates, tips and all of the latest news and be introduced to a whole raft of new opportunities and other entrepreneurs. There'll be

Live BIG. Think LARGE. Act SENSIBLY.
How to make a fortune - without losing your friends!

chances for you to joint venture, swap notes, share ideas and find out information.

Got an idea? Then let's see if together we can get it working for you in all of the ways you have imagined. Write me, email me or call me and together we'll work something out to get your idea(s) off the ground.

To succeed in life, as I've tried to show in this book, you have to start by knowing where to look. It can take you a long time, even a lifetime, to find the right resources that can help you to reach your dreams ... quickly.

I am confident that a good many of those resources are already in my corner and they are available to you, if and whenever you choose to use them.

But now I'm going to make a toast to your success. May it start brightly, accelerate swiftly and deliver massive quantities of consistent profits.

I dedicate my book to you, in friendship and belief.

"No dreamer is ever too small; no dream is ever too big."
Anonymous

"It is never too late to be who you might have been."
George Elliot (pen name of Mary Anne Evans), English novelist and leading writer of the Victorian era, 1819 -1880

FREE audio CD, especially FOR YOU!

This is How the World Works!

Some of what I have covered in this book and much more besides is expanded upon in my free audio CD which is called *This is How the World Works!*

It's full of riveting stuff about what you can do - *and how* - to make the world ... your world ... work just the way you've always wanted it to. You've read the book. Now here's a CD that will help you to make it all happen.

You can claim your FREE CD simply by visiting this website:

www.nick-james.com/howtheworldworks

Or, if you prefer, just send me an email to: nick@nick-james.com

(Please remember to add your name and address so that I know where to send your free CD!)

Perhaps you'd rather drop me a note or send a postcard with your name and address details to: Nick James, Power-Tech Associates Limited, 5 Forest Court, Oaklands Park, Wokingham, Berkshire, RG41 2FD, United Kingdom.

Whichever contact method you choose to use, there's a free CD waiting here, just for you.

Together, we can take things further.